CW00959469

After studying philosophy, psychology and sociology at Cologne University and Japanology and Sinology at the Free University of West Berlin Stephan Schuhmacher went to Japan in 1970 where he continued his studies at the Jesuite Sophia University, before he left the academic world to dedicate himself entirely to Zen practice. From 1970 to 1975 he practised Zen in the Sambō Kyōdan tradition under the guidance of Yasutani Hakuun Rōshi and Yamada Kōun Rōshi. While living in Japan, he translated the poetry of the 7th-century Chinese 'dharma bum' Hanshan (Cold Mountain) from Chinese into German and later the poetry of the great Tang period poet Wang Wei. He worked in publishing in Germany for many years, translated more than sixty works from all spiritual traditions into German, and edited and co-authored a dictionary of Eastern Wisdom that was translated into eight languages, in English it was published as the *Shambhala/Rider Encyclopedia of Eastern Philosophy and Religion*.

By the same author

Han Shan, 150 Gedichte vom Kalten Berg
(Reissued as: *Hanshan, Gedichte vom Kalten Berg*)

Wang Wei, Jenseits der weißen Wolken. Die Gedichte des Weisen vom Südgebirge

Writing as Michael S Diener
Das Lexikon des Zen

Contributor on Zen to:
The Rider Encyclopedia of Eastern Philosophy and Religion (Published in the US as *The Shambhala Encyclopedia of Eastern Philosophy and Religion*)

The Shambhala Dictionary of Buddhism and Zen (with Ingrid Fischer Schreiber and Franz-Karl Ehrhard)

ZEN

IN PLAIN ENGLISH

EXPERIENCE THE ESSENCE OF ZEN

STEPHAN SCHUHMACHER

WATKINS PUBLISHING
LONDON

This edition published in the UK 2009 by
Watkins Publishing, Sixth Floor, Castle House,
75–76 Wells Street, London W1T 3QH

Where not attributed to other sources the quotations in the text are the author's own translation. The Publisher wishes to thank all copyright holders who have kindly given permission for an extract to appear. If, however there are any omissions, the publisher will be pleased to correct the matter in any future editions.

1 3 5 7 9 10 8 6 4 2

Designed and typeset by Jerry Goldie Graphic Design

Printed and bound in WS Bookwell Oy

British Library Cataloguing-in-Publication data available

ISBN: 978-1-906787-20-2

www.watkinspublishing.co.uk

CONTENTS

This book is dedicated to my late Zen master, Kōun-an Chikō Rōshi (Brigitte D'Ortschy), *dharma* heir of Yasutani Hakuun Rōshi and Yamada Kōun Rōshi, who also were my first Zen masters. I had the great privilege to be not only a bad disciple of Kōun-an Chikō for 15 years, but also a good friend of hers for two decades. During this time, her example and her guidance, inspired by the unrelenting spirit of the patriarchal Chan masters of old, have penetrated my being to the core. Much of what she taught me has permeated my heart-mind to such an extent, that after nearly 20 years of continued practice since her death, it now feels to me as if mother and son are singing with one mouth. In this book I play, in my amateur way, a song that I have heard from her, and like a jazz musician, I am improvising on her melody. Thus, my very own melody would not exist without hers, and in this sense is altogether due to her. My gratitude for her loving guidance and ruthless compassion is deeper than anything that could be expressed here in words.

Stephan Schuhmacher,
in the 'Abode of the White Clouds',
Southern France

ACKNOWLEDGEMENTS

My gratitude goes out to a few friends in the *dharma* who helped to bring about the English edition of this book with words and deeds.

Thanks go to Joan Wulfsohn and Deborah Sanchez, who were kind enough to read the first draft of my own rendering of the German original into English. They suggested many helpful formal corrections.

Michael Mann, a long-time companion in the world of publishing, suggested the book to the publisher and brought about a contract. Thank you, Michael.

My dear friend Gerald Benedict Phillipson, an award-winning author of prose, graciously consented to edit the final draft of the manuscript and to transform my 'Germanenglish' into plain English. I thoroughly enjoyed the process of polishing up the style of my writing together with him during many hours of playful exploration of the layers of meaning hidden between the lines. I am grateful for his dedicated editorial work and for his willingness to accept my reluctance to *explain* where I intended to *challenge*.

When I met Peter Matthiessen (Muryō Rōshi) many years ago in his home on Long Island, it felt like meeting a 'kindred heart-mind' in the world of Western Zen.

I am most grateful to him for making the time to read the finished manuscript amidst the whirl of activities occasioned by his winning the American Book Award for the second time last year. My thanks go to him for supporting the publication of this book by contributing a short endorsement.

It all began in Kamakura, where Yasutani Hakuun Rōshi first demonstrated the possibility of direct communication from heart-mind to heart-mind to me, and where Yamada Kōun Rōshi not only guided the first years of my journey on the path of Zen, but also extended his generous hospitality and almost parental care on many occasions. I am grateful for their inspiration and guidance, which laid the foundation.

And it all led up to my encounter with Kōun-an Chikō Rōshi (Brigitte D'Ortschy) and more than 15 years of Zen training with her. Her guidance never ended, even after her departure from what she used to call her 'shabby winter coat'. When I want to express what I owe to her, all words seem futile. But she would know – like she always knew, what I could not say, what I did not say, and what could not be said.

PRELUDE

or

The Question of Life and Death

The question of life and death is momentous,

Therefore be sparing of your time ...

Beginning of a reminder of essentials,
recited in a Zen monastery at bedtime

This book is a presentation of Chan or Zen from the perspective of Zen.[1] It is not an account of facts and events which occurred in the distant past, a record that is merely meant to be correct from the point of view of an academic understanding of history. A historical approach, helpful as it may be for an understanding of the development of the outward form, misses the very essence of Zen – and one should not forget that it is one of the characteristics of Zen to steer as directly as possible, towards the essential.

If people approach a path of spiritual training, they do so in general because they hope to find answers to deepest existential questions: Who am I? What are life and death? What is the meaning of life? And if a person may be willing to undergo years, or even decades of a training discipline as demanding as Zen practice (as we shall see, it requires us to give all that we have, and even a little more) this warrants the assumption that she or he is looking for more than a merely intellectual answer.

The quest is for a solution, something that resolves and dissolves the deepest existential anxieties and distresses that are associated with the question of life and death and *my own tangible life* – not some philosophical abstraction. At stake is the dissolution of the knots in heart and mind, of the chronic cramp that prevents us from breathing freely, from giving ourselves without reserve to life in all its delightful and painful facets, and from being at peace with life and with death.

If for a person living in our modern Western world the confrontation with Zen is to be more than an intellectual pastime, the question cannot be under what conditions, historical, social and cultural, some enlightened Asian has said and done this or that, any number of centuries ago in India, China, Korea or Japan. Whoever expects to penetrate into the core of Zen by questions like these, may find himself in the position of the man, in a famous parable by the Buddha, who was wounded by an arrow: Before he allows a physician to remove the potentially lethal projectile from the wound, he demands to know who aimed the arrow at him, what age the archer has, what caste he belongs to and so forth. And thus he dies from the arrow even before he can be helped.

However, we all carry a lethal arrow in our flesh, that of ignorance with regard to our essential immortality, which is our *unborn-ness*. If we do not allow great physicians like the Buddha, or the masters of Zen to help us, we may not only die before we have resolved the question of life and death, *we may die before we have really lived*. The question thus is: What could the Zen tradition mean to every single one of us, existentially, here and now. Can it help *me* to find *my* solution?

It only can do so if it is more than history, if it transmits a truth that is independent of historical circumstances. And indeed, what is transmitted by the Zen tradition is a truth of a different order than that of the historical truth of the scholars. Likewise, it is completely irrelevant to the essential truth of Laozi's *Daodejing* whether there ever existed a single historical figure called Laozi (the 'Old Master') who was the author of this work. 'Laozi lives!'– his legend is quite real, since he has effectively inspired generations of seekers on their path of realization.

For that matter, the Zen tradition does not tell stories in order to write history, but to have an effect on us, to trigger something in us at *this* present moment in time. Over the centuries the masters of Chan have developed and used the art of storytelling as a cunning device (or as Buddhists would rather say, as a 'skilful means'), a method of shoving something under our nose that is always already openly visible but that we, nevertheless, did not perceive. That is why we are going to tell these stories here as they are told in the tradition – without the doubtful 'allegedly has' or 'is supposed to be' that is the trademark of the academic professional.

The stories that the masters of Zen tell do not provide us with answers to the question of the meaning of it all, they do not promise a magic formula for love, peace and happiness. They do not teach a 'moral of the tale', and they do not instruct us about stages of meditative absorption and other details of a technology of enlightenment. The masters do not make it all that comfortable for us to take home (only for it to gather dust on a chest of drawers) what, as Goethe said, we imagine to 'have down in black and white'. Instead they treat us to a meal that is indigestible for our categorizing intellect, for our discursive thought, or for our reason that while being so helpful in many respects in daily life, is so utterly helpless in existential matters. Instead, they say, 'Eat or die!' … or rather, 'Eat *and* die!'

They dare us to die the Great Death so that we come to know the Great Birth and discover through our own direct experience what the Buddha realized beneath the Bodhi Tree; why Bodhidharma came from the West; how to go on from the top of a 100-foot-high pole; whether each day can indeed be a good day; and what is the sound of one hand clapping.

> The fish trap exists because of the fish; once you've caught the fish, you can forget the trap. The rabbit snare exists because of the rabbit; once you've caught the rabbit, you can forget the snare. Words exist because of their meaning; once you have grasped the meaning, you can forget the words. Where can I find a man who knows how to forget about words so I can have a word with him?
>
> *Zhuangzi*, XXVI

1

THE FREEDOM OF THE LOSERS

or

Buddha's Enlightenment and the Roots of Zen in India

Freedom's just another word

for nothing left to lose.

Janis Joplin

The history of Zen begins with a loser, a guy who, despite his ideal circumstances, achieved 'nothing' by all the standards of our society.

Even if the cultural framework of his life looked somewhat different from our present occidental world, his existential situation was comparable to that of many members of our modern consumer society. He was the son of privileged parents, and grew up as a pampered boy under circumstances that left nothing to be desired. Even as a young man he already possessed all that one needs in order to be considered someone who has 'made it'. He was rich, he had a beautiful house, he enjoyed all the privileges of power, and knew all sensual pleasures, he had a beautiful young wife and a healthy son … what more could one demand?

And yet this ungrateful fellow was not content, not in peace. He was driven by a nagging feeling of doubt, a discontent that undermined his days. He was haunted by the archetypal bugbear of all those, who have *made it* – a question that could not be silenced: 'Can THIS really be all?' Money, status, power, sex, security … and then what? And then there is the painful first-hand confirmation of the truism, that all these things do not make you happy, that they do not even quiet the nerves.

How could anyone live in peace knowing with certainty that material security is an illusion; that you cannot escape illness, old age and death; that sooner or later – at the latest on your deathbed – you have to let go of *everything* that you cling to? Is there nowhere out there or maybe even deep inside *something* in which true happiness, real security, lasting peace can be found? Something, which is really worthwhile striving for, since it cannot be lost, because it is subject to neither death nor birth?

THE SEARCH

The story of the young man who went on a quest for this 'something' – the princess, the pearl, the treasure of all the fairytales and all mythology – the story of the prince Siddhārtha, has become sufficiently well known even in the West and needs not be recounted here in detail. He 'dropped out', he became a homeless mendicant, he renounced all the securities of the world of those who have made it. Really, all of them?

He became a tramp, a nobody for high society, a have-not ... but he still had the comforting feeling of belonging to the elite of those few who are destined for a higher cause than the common mass of man – an inner certainty that can enable one to bear many a hardship. Even in complete poverty he could still achieve something; namely knowledge, wisdom, enlightenment. After all, he lived in a society that – contrary to our own – held the quest for truth, the striving for transcendence of all worldly matters in great esteem. He had only to find the proper teachings, the right religion, the accomplished guru who would reveal to him 'the truth'.

Thus he wandered from one sage, one guru and one meditation workshop to the next. In the India of 2,500 years ago, the market in doctrines of salvation and wisdom teachings was by no means as colourful and variegated as the occidental spiritual supermarket of our days. Still, it offered a rich variety of divergent teachings and practices that were supposed to lead to inner peace. Siddhārtha tried them all assiduously. He was willing

Siddhārtha Gautama (approximately 563–483 BC), northern Indian prince from the house of Shākya. At the age of 29 he left his wife and son and the palace of his father Suddhodana, who wanted him to succeed him as ruler, and became a 'homeless' mendicant. He studied and practised with many different ascetic teachers without achieving his goal, inner liberation. Only when he took up the practice of meditation, at the age of 35, did he finally achieve awakening or enlightenment (Skrt. *bodhi*) sitting under the so-called Bodhi Tree. Thus he became the 'Buddha', that is, 'the Awakened One', and is considered the historical Buddha of our age.

to get really involved, to be disciplined, focused, and to 'work' seriously on himself. He was not so naïve as to believe that you only have to pick up the proper jargon, the right ideology to belong to those who have made it spiritually.

Siddhārtha not only studied the words of sages, he also learned to perform complicated rites; he studied the yogic mastery of the body, he practised breathing and meditation, he underwent the strictest asceticism and fasted until he was on the verge of physical death.

He did everything one could demand of someone on the quest for truth, and because of his exemplary striving he became known among his companions as the 'silent ascetic from the house of Shākya'. At that time he probably had quite a number of peak experiences. Depending with which guru he was presently studying, and which spiritual practices he was presently performing, he probably experienced shamanistic spirit journeys, meditative trances, and mystical states of rapture. But he did not find deep and lasting inner peace. Any state that he could 'achieve', he could also lose again.

Thus at the age of 35 he had reached a dead end: He had tried everything to the best of his abilities – and he had achieved nothing. He had long since realized that 'worldly' achievements and pleasures are not satisfactory in the long run, *cannot* be satisfactory – and had renounced them. But ever since the quest itself, the conviction that he was on the path to enlightenment imparted a certain meaning to his solitary life as one who is neither at home in society, nor in one of the established religions, nor in one of the many spiritual communities who sneer at established religion. Now he began to have his doubts about the search itself, about the quest for the enlightening truth.

FINDING

What had all his searching with total commitment of body, mind and soul finally earned him? Nothing – at least no lasting peace. Was the path *really* the goal? Was it even possible at all to reach his goal as long as he was still convinced of being on the path *towards* it? After all that he had already renounced and lost, was it perhaps necessary also to lose this last hope for salvation, for liberation, for enlightenment? Nobody could give him a satisfactory answer to his questions. He himself could find none. He had invested everything that was physically, emotionally, intellectually and even intuitively within his power. Now he could do no more. *He was at the end of his wits – and thus at the beginning of Zen.*

And so he gave up searching. Well, maybe he did not even *do* that. Maybe it just happened by itself, because he was fed up with the world, with himself, with the search, with *everything* – he had just had it. Thus he sat down under a tree, completely absorbed – that is not existing any more as somebody who could do or wanted to do anything – and just *did nothing at all*. Later it was reported that he sat down under the so-called Bodhi Tree in the north Indian village of

Bodh-Gāyā with the firm resolve not to get up again before he had attained complete enlightenment. This may be true. But whether before or after his sitting down – and some sources say that he 'sat' there not less than six years – at some time he must have reached a point where all hope and fear, all striving and searching, all wanting and doing simply dropped away – or else what happened next could not have happened.

What it was, that happened, is described by the Denkōroku, the 'Record of the Transmission of the Light', in one short sentence:

> On seeing the morning star Shākyamuni Buddha realized enlightenment and said, 'I and the Great Earth and all sentient beings simultaneously attain enlightenment.'

Not more and not less! Shākyamuni, the 'sage' or the 'silent ascetic' from the house of Shākya had become Shākyamuni Buddha, 'Shākyamuni the Awakened'. Awakened from what? To what? What had he realized? The first sentence that he uttered after his perfect enlightenment – his first 'lion's roar' – already discloses all that can be disclosed, 'I and the Great Earth [the whole universe] and all sentient beings simultaneously attain enlightenment'. And interestingly enough he says 'attain' and not 'have attained', since it is not an event that has happened in the past, but it is still happening, even now, all of the time and beyond any time in the eternal now.

But of course nobody believed him, even as he himself would not have believed this statement and could not have believed it before he forfeited all searching. And that is why until today, 2,500 years after Shākyamuni Buddha, we still have a 'path of awakening' that was first called *dhyāna*, absorption or meditation, in India, and later on in China (as a phonetic transcription of *dhyāna*) *channa* or *chan,* and finally in Japan *zenna,* or *zen*. It is a path of spiritual training that essentially is modelled on the inner path and the arrival of the historic Buddha Shākyamuni.

Those who practise learning

Gain something day by day.

Those who practise the Way,

Lose something day by day.

They lose and even lose losing,

Until they arrive at non-doing,

The non-doing in which

Nothing is left undone.

Laozi, a contemporary of Shākyamuni Buddha and one of the forefathers of Chan in the *Daodejing*

2

THE TREASURE OF THE ANCIENT MASTERS

or

What is It, That is 'Transmitted' in Zen?

Dazhu Huihai came to see Master Mazu.

Mazu asked him, "What do you come here for?"

Dazhu replied, "I am coming, because I am striving for enlightenment."

The master said, "Why do you leave your home and wander around despising your own precious treasure? There is nothing I could give you. Why do you come looking for enlightenment with me?"

Dazhu asked, "But what is my own treasure?"

The master replied, "It is just the one who is asking this question right now. He encompasses everything and he lacks nothing. Thus it is not necessary to look outside of yourself."

From the *Jingde chuandenglu*, the 'Record of the Passing On of the Lamp, compiled in the Jingde era'

Had Shākyamuni *attained* something after all? At least he was a Buddha now, an Awakened One or Enlightened One. For many of those who encountered him after his great experience under the Bodhi Tree, this was beyond doubt. To them there was no question that this man, who suddenly emanated such an extraordinary serenity and clarity, such an unshakable certainty, such an exceptional inner peace, had to 'have' something that others had not! Certainly one could get something from a person who obviously possessed something so very precious.

This is how Siddhārtha Gautama, who had been disillusioned with all gurus during his own search for the Great Treasure, finally became a guru himself. More and more treasure hunters gathered around him, people who were on a quest for knowledge, wisdom and enlightenment and who were – well, at least some of them were – ready to really get 'involved'. We already know the knitting pattern of the story, and it will henceforth be repeated countless times. This is the eternal story of searchers who hope that the 'enlightened teacher' will hand over something to them that they themselves believe they do not possess – those who wanted the Buddha to *share* the treasure he had found himself, with them. But what did this treasure consist of?

THE ZEN TEACHING OF THE AWAKENED ONE

Once, the Buddha stayed on the mountain Gridhrakūta, the 'Vulture Peak'. There 80,000 treasure hunters had gathered around him and waited for an exposition of his enlightened understanding; a 'teaching' as contemporary Buddhist jargon would have it. And not unlike the participants in modern-day 'Meditation Workshops', many of the 80,000 disciples, students and followers had, so to say, their pencils sharpened and their tape recorders on record so as to be able to take something home at night, some words of wisdom that would inspire and uplift their minds (or that would serve to make an impression in a discussion ... of course only with spiritually minded people!). They were waiting for instructions in some kind of esoteric practice that would guarantee the practitioner this or that state of meditative absorption, maybe even for some form of, as yet, 'secret' initiation. The 'Record of the Transmission of the Light' reports:

> Once, the World-honoured One [Shākyamuni Buddha] held up a flower and blinked his eyes. Kāshyapa broke out in a smile. The World-honoured One said, 'I have the

> Treasury of the Eye of the True Dharma, the ineffable mind of *nirvāna*. I entrust it to Mahākāshyapa.'

In different texts from different centuries one finds slightly divergent versions of this story that, according to the tradition of Zen, tells of the transmission of the 'True Dharma', the essential truth of Buddhism, to the first patriarch (in the Indian lineage) of Zen. Each version that moves us to break out in the smile of Kāshyapa is true. For several subtle reasons, the above version is particularly revealing.

Kāshyapa in the end has become Mahākāshyapa, the 'Great Kāshyapa'; apparently he underwent a thorough transformation. Kāshyapa *breaks out* in a smile; obviously he has suddenly comprehended something. The shock and the joy of this sudden comprehension, as well as his inspired and delighted agreement with the eloquent discourse the World-honoured One has just delivered, manifested in this radiant and liberated smile. And since Kāshyapa has comprehended, the Buddha now can entrust him with the responsibility to carry on what he himself has comprehended.

Now this clear and penetrating comprehension, the 'Treasury of the Eye of the True Dharma', unfortunately

Dharma – a Sanskrit term (literally, 'that which carries or holds') with multiple meanings, that in Zen is used predominantly in the following three senses:

1 The one, absolute, nondual reality.
2 The 'cosmic law', the 'Great Order' that underlies our phenomenal world, especially the karmic law of cause and effect.
3 The teaching of the Buddha who has realized this 'law' and has comprehended and formulated the basic unity of absolute (1) and relative (2) reality.

While 'Buddhism' is a term coined in the West, the teaching of the Buddha is called the *buddhadharma* in the East, that is, the teaching of the Enlightened One that expresses the universal truth. In this sense the *dharma* exists 'eternally', i.e. beyond time, and the historic Buddha Shākyamuni is only one of countless expressions thereof.

is (and this is the problem for all those who are, their pencils whipped out, still waiting for some sublime truth from the lips of the World-honoured One) as ineffable as the deep peace, the *nirvāna*, that goes along with it. With regard to the essential content of the experience of awakening, the Zen tradition holds that an Awakened One is like 'a mute who has had a dream'. And finally there is nothing, not even something ineffable or unspeakable that could be 'transmitted', that could be handed on from here to there in time and space. The Chan master Huangbo, who has realized this awakening himself, says about this treasure:

> Our original *buddha-nature* is, in highest truth, devoid of any atom of objectivity. It is void, omnipresent, silent, pure; it is glorious and mysterious peaceful joy – and that is all. Enter deeply into it by awakening to it yourself. That which is before you is it, in all its fullness, utterly complete. There is naught beside. Even if you go through all the stages of a Bodhisattva's progress towards Buddhahood, one by one; when at last, in a single flash, you attain to full realization, you will only be realizing the *buddha-nature* which has been with you all the time; and by all the foregoing stages you will have added to it nothing at all. You will come to look upon

> those aeons of work and achievement as no better than unreal actions performed in a dream. That is why the Tathāgata [Buddha Shākyamuni] said, 'I truly attained nothing from complete, unexcelled enlightenment.'[2]

So, there is nothing the Buddha has 'attained' and that he could 'give' to Kāshyapa. There only is what is, and what always has been and always will be – and it is *thus*, exactly as it is: a simple fact. And to see what *is*, really is

A ***kalpa*** according to Hindu-Buddhist cosmology is a world cycle of immense duration, the time that elapses between the creation, the dissolution and the recreation of the cosmos. In unbroken continuity, without beginning or end, myriads of worlds are created and perish again in a great cosmic fire. The Indian tradition gives the following simile for the unimaginable duration of one *kalpa*:

If an angel slightly touches a gigantic mountain of granite with a silk scarf once in a hundred years, it would take a *kalpa* to completely wear down the mountain.

no great achievement … or is it? There is a flower. The Buddha is blinking his eyes. *Off – On. Off – On.* Moment by Moment, *kalpa* by *kalpa* – just this! A flower, in the annihilation of the cosmos and in the re-creation of the cosmos, beyond becoming and cessation, beyond any time within which something could be transmitted: just this! A rose is a rose is a rose …

Nevertheless, this exchange between the historic Buddha Shākyamuni and Mahākāshyapa, one of his closest disciples, is considered to be the beginning of the 'transmission of the light' within the 'lineage of the transmission of Zen' that spans 2,500 years from the historic Buddha to our present time. What should we make of that?

THE PROBLEM OF 'TRANSMISSION'

If we are to believe the academic scholars of Buddhism, the lineage of Zen transmission, especially that of the early Indian patriarchs, is a fake, a defensive lie. It is born out of the attempt by later Zen teachers, to justify their own claim to be authentic descendants of the Buddha through a lineage that was artificially constructed, *a posteriori*, to demonstrate an uninterrupted

The **28 patriarchs** following the Buddha Shākyamuni **in the Indian lineage** of the transmission of Zen:

1. Mahākāshyapa	15. Kānadeva
2. Ānanda	16. Rāhulabhadra
3. Shānavasin	17. Samghanandi
4. Upagupta	18. Samghayathata
5. Dhītika	19. Kumā ralāta
6. Mishaka	20. Shayata
7. Vasumitra	21. Vasubandhu
8. Buddhanandi	22. Manorata
9. Buddhamitra	23. Haklenayasha
10. Pārshva	24. Simhabodhi
11. Punyayasha	25. Bashashita
12. Ānabodhi	26. Punyamitra
13. Kapimala	27. Prajñādhāra
14. Nāgārjuna	28. Bodhidharma

chain of 'transmission of the light', from the historic Buddha to themselves. From a historic point of view this may not even be completely erroneous. Wherever living spiritual traditions were institutionalized they became petrified and more often than not ended up as dead religious organizations. These organizations often used cosmetic corrections of the historical truth to justify the privileged position of their clergy. And even traditions that are as fervently opposed to institutionalization as the so-called Chan Buddhism and Zen Buddhism have, in the course of their history, not been spared the trappings of this tendency.

But with a mere historical understanding of the transmission in Zen, the scholarly Buddhologists (and not only them) miss by far the *essential* truth of what the Awakened One taught. These Buddhologists also fail to understand the essence of Chan, or Zen, as a gateway to awakening. As a result, they completely miss the reality and the pivotal meaning of awakening itself!

That is to say, whoever realizes this awakening is able, (as the Chan master Wumen Huikai says in the *Wumenguan*, 'The Barrier Without Gate') 'to walk hand in hand with the whole descending line of Chan masters and be eyebrow to eyebrow with them. He can see with the same eyes they see with, hear with the same ear they hear with.' Mind you, not with *similar* eyes but with the *same* eyes!

Transmission happens beyond (or rather on this side of) time and space in the eternal now. And it does not reach over thousands of miles from India to China,

Korea and Japan and finally to the modern West, but it happens in the dimensionless point of the here and now. Once this is understood, the respective patriarchs in the official lineage of transmission of Zen are seen as nothing but historical *examples* of the ahistoric, eternal (and that means timeless) principle of awakening. This principle has been actualized by beings in all generations since the advent of the historic Buddha (and even before). In their awakened *buddha-nature* the patriarchs stand 'eyebrow to eyebrow', without a 'before' or an 'after' in this dimensionless eternal moment.

This is why the Japanese Zen master Keizan (who has compiled the Denkōroku or 'Record of the Transmission of the Light' and has written commentaries on the respective transmission stories collected therein), says in his discourse on the case of the transmission from Shākyamuni to Mahākāshyapa:

> If you can reach this place, then you will be a successor to Kāshyapa, and Kāshyapa will receive [the true law] from you. Not only does it come down to you from the seven [past] Buddhas, but you will be able to be the patriarchal teacher of the seven Buddhas. Beginningless and endless, annihilating past

> and present, here is the abiding place of the entrusting of the Treasury of the Eye of the True Dharma.[3]

But then again, if the Buddha himself had not attained anything, what then could he teach? If the True Dharma is ineffable and unspeakable and there is nothing (of essential importance) that could be handed down, to what end is all that talk about the tradition of Zen and the 'transmission of the light?' In the *Wumenguan* (case 42) Master Wumen commenting on the efforts of the World-honoured One to teach and to hand down the True Dharma, writes, 'The old Shākya is staging a rural farce.' But this knockabout comedy seems to have pleased the country dolts called Zen patriarchs and masters so much, that they have continued the play and have been staging it again and again with different actors and in different sets.

We can count ourselves lucky that they have done so, because it is good that, even now, we get an occasion to laugh – or maybe even to smile.

"So!" said the Old Master, "If the Way could be presented, then everyone would present it to his lord. If the Way could be offered, then everybody would offer it to his parents. If the Way could be told, then everyone would tell it to his brothers. If the way could be given, then everybody would give it to his descendants."

Zhuangzi XIV.5
as translated by Victor Mair

3

WHY BODHIDHARMA CAME FROM THE WEST

or

How Zen Travelled from India to China

High, high up on the loftiest peak,
All around nothing but open vastness.
Sitting alone where no man knows,
The lone moon is mirrored in a cold spring.
But in the spring that is not the moon,
The moon itself is in the black sky.
I sing this awkward little song for you,
However in this song there is no Zen

Hanshan

About 1,000 years after Buddha Shākyamuni and Mahākāshyapa, an enigmatic stranger disembarked from a ship in southern China. He came from India, which for Chinese people was situated in 'the west'. And since the Chinese of those days, not different from most people all over the world even today, considered their own village the centre of the universe and regarded everything and everybody alien to them with suspicion, he became known among them by the nickname 'Barbarian from the West'.

Countless Zen paintings from later centuries depict him as an imposing figure with a thick black beard, bushy eyebrows, bulging lips, a penetrating gaze, a ring in one earlobe and a grim, nearly frightening expression, a guy you would not like to encounter alone in a dark alley. His looks were more likely those of a pirate or a highwayman; not those of the 'Buddhist monk' he pretended to be. And indeed he turned out to be a robber, one who stole from at least one Chinaman everything this poor chap possessed, even the concept of his own identity that was basic for the survival of his ego. But isn't it just typical of Zen, that of all people, a highwayman, named Bodhidharma – being the 28th Indian patriarch in the lineage of transmission of the True Dharma that began with Mahākāshyapa – actually became the first patriarch in the Chinese lineage of Chan.

When he arrived at the port of Canton in southern China he was but one among many Buddhist monks from India who had come to China during the past centuries. From the 1st century CE, these monks had spread the *buddhadharma* there by (among other activities) their cooperation in groundbreaking translations of the holy scriptures of Buddhism. These were mainly the outstanding *sūtras* of the *Mahāyāna*, the 'Greater Vehicle', as the stream of Buddhist teaching and practice was called, by which Bodhidharma himself was carried to the shores of China. These initiatives had already led to the first heyday of Buddhism in China one century before the arrival of Bodhidharma.

Now, as we will later see, the 'Barbarian from the West' did not really distinguish himself by particular missionary fervour. In fact he does not seem to have made much ado about himself in any respect. Still, much as Shākyamuni Buddha once did, he emanated *something* that made people suspect he possessed some kind of treasure. The rumour spread and reached the Emperor Wu of the Liang dynasty, who was reigning in southern China. The emperor thus invited Bodhidharma to his court to expound his understanding of

Mahāyāna (literally: 'Great(er) Vehicle', one of the major schools of Buddhism, prevalent in East Asia, mainly China, Korea and Japan. The other two schools being Theravāda, the 'Way of the Elders' (called Hīnayāna or 'Lesser Vehicle' by the followers of Mahayana), prevalent in Southeast Asia, and Vajrayāna, the 'Diamond Vehicle', prevalent in Central Asia, mainly Tibet, Bhutan, Mongolia.

The ideal of the Mahayana is the **Bodhisattva** ('Enlightenment Being') who renounces complete entry into *nirvāna* ('cessation') and vows to remain in the cycle of existence and to work for the good of all sentient beings until they are saved, i.e. have themselves attained enlightenment or awakening. The doctrine of the Mahayana is based mainly on those ***sūtras*** (scriptures attributed to the Buddha) that were probably composed between the 1st century BCE and the 6th century CE. Some Mahayana *sūtras*, like the *Lankāvatāra-sūtra* ,played a certain role in early Chan, although this tradition generally stresses that it is 'independent of holy scriptures'.

the Buddhist 'religion' there – and Bodhidharma thoroughly complied with this request.

A RELIGION WITHOUT HOLINESS

The Emperor Wu had already contributed a lot to establishing the lofty doctrine of the *buddhadharma* in China; he had sponsored Buddhist masters and had built several monasteries. He even had himself ordained as a Buddhist monk and had some experience in meditation. Thus he considered himself a seasoned Buddhist and was convinced that he had earned at least an auspicious rebirth with all the good karma he had amassed – if not, perhaps, also a little enlightenment. But certainly he merited the approval and recognition of a mendicant monk from the homeland of the Buddha. He therefore asked Bodhidharma at their first encounter: "We have built monasteries and had monks ordained; what merit have we gained therewith?"

This was *the* chance for Bodhidharma to perhaps be appointed abbot of one of the monasteries patronized by the emperor, and thus to be sitting pretty for the rest of his life. All he needed to do now was to butter up the emperor a little bit and he might have established himself (even if he was not interested in a position of material wealth and security) as the teacher of the emperor, and thus as *guoshi*, or 'teacher of the nation'. What a wonderful opportunity to render Buddhism and its dissemination in China an enormous service; why had he, after all, undertaken the arduous journey to China from the west? And what did he reply to the emperor's question? Two little words: "No merit."

Now what the heck – he obviously was a real barbarian. Not the least bit of politeness – imagine *that*! Just to remain true to the essential truth of the 'Treasury of the Eye of the True Dharma' he risks his neck and hurls these two little words at the emperor. He might have literally lost his head, but this didn't seem to bother him. Maybe this Barbarian from the West really did have something very special to offer, something that transcended the orthodox teaching of cause and effect, of good deeds and the merit acquired therewith?

The emperor seemed to be impressed, and he had enough style to give Bodhidharma a second chance. But this time he would not settle for peanuts – for a few appreciative words, or for a teaching on the karmic consequences of good deeds. This time, Bodhidharma would have to reveal all. The emperor wanted him to open up his chest, his treasury, and hand over the pearl of the True Dharma. In the classic *Biyanlu*, the 'Blue Cliff Record' we hear:

> Emperor Wu of Liang asked Bodhidharma:
> "What is the highest meaning of the holy truth?"
> Bodhidharma said: "Vast emptiness – nothing holy."

Bang! One more clip round the ears! Here we have this seemingly uncivilized hobo from the west telling the emperor of China that all his ideas about the lofty doctrine of Buddhism, of something holy, that transcends despicable profane reality, are erroneous, that they simply miss the point of the true nature of reality, that they are completely off the mark. And so also is the belief in a 'holy truth', the highest meaning of which can be *shared*, can be imparted to others in monasteries and other institutions: "Well, you know, according to chapter X, Y and Z of this and that record of the authentic words of the Great Enlightened Being Shākyamuni Buddha, the highest meaning of the holy truth is the following …" Or did Bodhidharma really offer the pearl to Emperor Wu on the palm of his hand, and the emperor simply did not know how to grasp it?

The emperor was beginning to have his doubts about this strange guy. Who did he think he was, daring to behave in such an unruly manner? If he expected to get away with this, he would have to present proof of some *real* credentials, maybe some diploma from an esoteric school of Buddhism completely unknown in China. Thus the emperor continued to inquire: "Who is it in front of me?" Now, finally Bodhidharma might have saved the situation for the good of his 'doctrine' by divulging to the emperor that he was the 28th patriarch of a school of Buddhism claiming to preserve and transmit the essence of the *buddhadharma*, which is awakening itself, the Treasury of the Eye of the True Dharma. Had he only explained the nature of Dhyāna Buddhism, of which he was an emissary, with the words that (probably) were put into his mouth by later generations:

> A special transmission outside orthodox
>   teaching:
> Not depending on sacred writings,
> And directly pointing to the human
>   heart-mind,
> It leads to the realization of one's own nature
>   and being a Buddha oneself.

Well, he might have, but as *we* might by now already suspect, he remained true to himself and was not into making any concessions to the mundane level of understanding of the emperor. And so he answered the question "Now *who* are you, mister, in front of me?" in his usual concise manner, speaking from the point of view of absolute truth: "(I) don't know."

Now the cat is out of the bag. He was an *ignoramus*! One who was 'lonely and poor' as Shākyamuni Buddha had been, one who did not possess anything any longer, and who had, by the experience of enlightenment, 'truly attained nothing' that he could have imparted to the emperor – and certainly not as long as the emperor had anyone 'in front of' him.

THE TEACHING WITHOUT WORDS

The rest of the story about Bodhidharma and the Emperor Wu of Liang is quickly told. The emperor did not understand or, as Katsuki Sekida says in his translation of Case One of the *Biyanlu* that relates this story – 'the emperor did not grasp his meaning'. This is why Bodhidharma proceeded to wander towards the north of China. He 'crossed the river' and finally settled down in

The **Shaolin monastery** (Chin. Shaolin si, Jap. Shōrin-ji) is a Buddhist monastery on the sacred mountain Song in today's Henan province; it was founded in the year 477 by the Emperor Xiaowen. In the early 6th century the Indian monk Bodhiruchi stayed here and translated several *sūtras* into Chinese. In the Zen tradition this monastery became known as the place where Bodhidharma sat in absorption for nine years 'facing the wall'.

According to legend, the **martial art** ***gongfu*** **(kung fu)** was developed by Buddhist monks in the Shaolin monastery. This is why adepts of this art like to relate *gongfu* to Zen. There are, however, no records in the Zen tradition indicating that one of the great Chan masters of old practised or taught martial arts.

the state of Wei in the vicinity of the Shaolin monastery.

Only later did it dawn on the Emperor Wu – who may have thought that Bodhidharma was just a poor madman and thus allowed him to depart with his head on his shoulders – that he had let a true treasure slip through his fingers. He wanted to send an emissary to invite Bodhidharma to return, but he had a counsellor who obviously had a clearer eye than the emperor and who advised him not to demean himself once more. "Your majesty had better not send someone to fetch him back. Even if the whole country were to run after him, he would not turn back."

Now, even if the urgent pleas of all the seekers in the country would not have persuaded the Barbarian from the West to come down to their level of understanding and 'teach' them something, the question has to be asked, what had he come to China for? *Why did Bodhidharma come from the West*? Ever since, this question has been echoing through the corridors and meditation halls of the Chan and Zen monasteries and in the minds of the practitioners of Zen. It has become a challenge to encounter Bodhidharma directly, in person, and to stand eyebrow to eyebrow with him in the 'vast emptiness'. Rather than having to settle for second-hand information about the True Dharma, the goal is to see with the same eyes and hear with the same ears as all the patriarchs.

And how can this intimacy with the patriarchs be realized? Maybe it was exactly by *not* teaching (and for that matter by not proselytizing) that Bodhidharma gave a clear indication of what is needed to meet with him and all the patriarchs, including Shākyamuni Buddha and the seven Buddhas of the past eons, in the dimensionless point of the transmission of the treasure. Let's have a look at what it was that he really did do. He sat down facing the wall in a cave near the Shaolin monastery and did ... *nothing*. He sat in silent absorption (*dhyāna*), *zuochan*, *zazen*). Nothing else. No discourses, no 'teachings', no initiations ... just this!

Some sources say that Shākyamuni sat for six years under the Bodhi Tree until his great awakening occurred, by which he 'truly attained nothing'. Bodhidharma 'sat' at Shaolin for nine years 'facing the wall' even after he had realized awakening. So is it that those who are following Shākyamuni Buddha, Mahākāshyapa and Bodhidharma on the path of Zen really practise *zazen* to attain enlightenment? And if you do not practise to attain anything, then why on earth do you practise? WHY did Bodhidharma come from the west?

On entering the assembly hall master Huangbo said:

"The possession of many kinds of knowledge is not comparable to the renouncement of searching for anything. This is the best of all things. There are no different kinds of Mind, and there is no teaching, that could be framed in words. Since there is nothing more to say, the assembly is closed."

From the *Yunzhou Huangbo Duanji Chanshi Yulu*,
the 'Record of the Sayings of Chan master
Huangbo Duanji of Yunzhou'

4

BUDDHA AND ZHUANGZI GO TO MARKET

or

Zen as the Offspring of the Marriage of Buddhism and Daoism

Korf invents a certain kind of joke

That catch on only hours after telling.

Boredom reigns when people hear them,

But as if some tinder had been glowing slowly,

One suddenly perks up in bed at midnight,

Blissfully smiling like a well-fed infant.

Christian Morgenstern

So Bodhidharma sat in front of the rocky wall of his cave and did nothing: no advertising, no meditation workshops, no congresses, no books and religious paraphernalia, no guru-hype. The Chinese sage Zhuangzi wrote, about 800 years before Bodhidharma came to China:

> The great Way is ineffable, great disputation is speechless, great humaneness is inhumane, great honesty is immodest and great bravery is not aggressive. The way that displays itself is not the Way. Speech that is disputatious fails to achieve its aims. Humaneness that is constant cannot go around. Honesty that is aloof will not be trusted. Bravery that is aggressive will not succeed. One who does not abandon these five precepts will be more or less headed in the right direction.
>
> Therefore she who knows to stop at what she does not know has attained the ultimate. Who knows the disputation that is without words and the Way that cannot be walked upon? If one can have knowledge of them, this is called the Treasury of Heaven. You may pour into it, but it never fills; you may dip

> from it, but it never empties; and you never know where it comes from. This is called the Inner Light.[4]

Had Bodhidharma at the court of Liang not encountered an ardent Buddhist stuck in the ruts of orthodox doctrine, but instead this old Daoist who knew how to catch the rabbit and forget the snare, then he 'could have had a word with him'. Zhuangzi would have comprehended his not-knowing. He would not have needed to ask him to open the Treasury of the Eye of the True Dharma and offer him a present. He would just have joined him in the vast emptiness, the luminous openness, the inexhaustible plenitude of the emptiness of the Inner Light, and the two of them would probably have gone to the next tavern to have a drink together – at any rate they would not have discussed how one could 'foster all living beings' (*see* page 60) and save the world.

But even though a transmission of the True Dharma had already existed in China for many centuries – a manifestation of the dharma that here was called 'Dao' – those days, like nowadays, there were few people who were ready to lose every thing to gain everything. And so by holding on to their possessions – their concepts, their knowledge, their certainties – the people around

Bodhidharma lived in great need. Why did the Barbarian from the West do nothing to relieve their misery? Why did he not point out to them the way to salvation and enlightenment? Did he not come from a tradition of the Mahayana, the 'Great Vehicle', that claimed to work for the salvation of all sentient beings? Are not the 'Four Great Vows' recited regularly in Zen monasteries and by all Zen practitioners everywhere up to our present day?

The **'Four Great Vows'**, a concise form of the bodhisattva vows, which are recited daily in Zen monasteries:

Sentient beings are countless – I vow to save them all.

Tormenting passions are innumerable – I vow to uproot them all.

The gates of the dharma are manifold – I vow to pass through them all.

The Buddha's way is unsurpassable – I vow to actualize it.

But what did Bodhidharma do to save all sentient beings? Well, maybe he was just living up to what the Buddha had proclaimed after his own awakening: 'I and the Great Earth and all sentient beings simultaneously attain enlightenment.' Maybe he did what was necessary by sitting in absorption, gazing at the wall, and thus deepening his own enlightenment and that of the Great Earth and all sentient beings encompassed by it. Maybe he was silently, but nevertheless eloquently, teaching the WAY for all those who have eyes to see, by manifesting his buddha-nature every instant of his sitting!

THE EARLY CHINESE PATRIARCHS

Actually Bodhidharma's non-doing at Shaolin was not mere idleness. It was the kind of non-doing that, as Laozi said, 'leaves nothing undone'. And so what had to happen came to pass. A treasure hunter by the name of Huike became aware of him ... well and then, of course, 'the same procedure as *every* generation', Act 29 of the Old Shakya's rural farce about transmission. The *Encyclopaedia of Eastern Philosophy and Religion* summarizes the plot of this act:

> According to tradition Hui-k'o [Huike] came to Shaolin monastery in about his fortieth year to ask Bodhidharma for instruction. It is said that initially Bodhidharma did not acknowledge him and Hui-k'o stood for several days in the snow in front of the cave where the first patriarch was practising *zazen* 'facing the wall'. In order to prove his earnestness to the Indian master of the *buddhadharma* and to induce the latter to accept him as student, Hui-k'o finally cut his own left arm off and presented it to Bodhidharma, who thereupon accepted him as a student.

Here we obviously had someone, who found himself in such burning inner need, and who was so much under the sway of suffering, that he was prepared to give everything to find the True Dharma, and thus inner peace. Bodhidharma just could not resist this overwhelming urge for truth, and so he consented to play along with him. Not that he tried to make it easy for Huike, and simply handed the pearl over to him, he knew that Huike would have to find it for himself. Huike, however, who had been searching with such intensity and who up to now had not found what he was searching for, obviously was already very close to giving (himself) up. All that was necessary in this state of urgency was a little nudge that would trigger a first breakthrough. According to case 41 of the *Wumenguan* it was the following dialogue that preceded this awakening and triggered it:

> Bodhidharma sat facing the wall. The Second Patriarch, who had been standing in the snow, cut his own arm off and said: "The heart-mind of your student has still found no peace. I entreat you, master, give it peace."
>
> Bodhidharma said: "Bring your heart-mind here, and I will pacify it."
>
> The Second Patriarch said: "I have searched for the heart-mind, but in the end it cannot be found."
>
> Bodhidharma said: "Then I have thoroughly pacified it."

After six years of further training, Bodhidharma entrusted Huike with the Treasury of the Eye of the True Dharma, and Huike thus became the second patriarch of Zen in China.

The **Chinese patriarchs of Zen** (after Huineng the status of patriarch was not conferred to one single dharma heir any more):

28th Indian and
1st Chinese patriarch: Bodhidharma (Chin.: Puti Damo, Jap. Bodai Daruma, ca. 470–543)
2nd patriarch: Dazu Huike (Jap. Taiso Eka, 487–595)
3rd patriarch: Jianzhi Sengcan (Jap. Kanchi Sōsan, died 606)
4th patriarch: Dayi Daoxin (Jap. Daii Dōshin, 580–651)
5th patriarch: Daman Hongren (Jap. Daiman Kōnin, 601–674)
6th patriarch: Dajian Huineng (Jap. Daikan Enō, 638–713)

Huike had been a reputed scholar, well versed in the writings of the 'Three Teachings' (Confucianism, Daoism and Buddhism) even before he encountered Bodhidharma, but had found no satisfaction in mere book learning, and thus had been yearning for a direct experience of the True Dharma. Following him, the enactment of transmission was continued by three further generations of dharma heirs up to a young man, who once again stood on the lowest rung of the ladder of social status. This man sets a new high-water mark in the annals of Zen as well as the end of the official transmission of the patriarchy in the tradition of Zen. We will come back to his story a little later.

FROM DHYĀNA BUDDHISM TO ZEN

With the confirmation of Huike as the second patriarch, the Dhyāna Buddhism of the forefathers of Bodhidharma now had, at least for the future historians of Zen Buddhism, arrived in China. Actually even before Bodhidharma there had been important exponents of Meditation Buddhism in China, and many of the doctrines that later were held to be 'typically Zen' had already been taught not only by Buddhist masters but also by the Dao heirs of Laozi and Zhuangzi. The overriding importance of meditation, what was called, absorption, or *dhyāna*, had been emphasized in Chinese Buddhism since the 2nd century CE, when An Shigao, translated some of the central *sūtras* of Indian Dhyāna Buddhism into Chinese, including the *sūtra* on, 'Absorption through Breath-Control'.

The Buddhist monk Kumārajīva came from Kucha, an oasis on the northern Silk Road which, in the early 5th century CE, had been an important centre of Buddhism on the trade route connecting India and China. He translated into Chinese important texts belonging to the *prajñāpāramitā* literature, such as the *sūtras* on 'the wisdom (*prajñā*) that reaches the further shore (*pāramitā*)'. He also translated commentaries on these texts which included those by Nāgārjuna, who is considered to be the 14th Indian patriarch in the Zen tradition. The core teachings on this liberating wisdom found their most concise expression in the so-called 'Heart Sūtra' (*Prajñāpāramitā-hridaya-sūtra*), the heart or core of the Great Wisdom Sūtra, that climaxes in the sentence, 'Form as such is emptiness; emptiness as such is form' and which is still recited in Zen monasteries today as a reminder of the central insight of the Eye of the True Dharma.

Sengzhao, one of the students of Kumārajīva, already expounded the doctrine of 'not-knowing' as true knowledge. In his text, 'On Prajñā Not Being Knowledge', he says:

> Because Wisdom is assumed to know what is to be known and to apprehend the qualities (of

> things), it is said to be knowledge. But since Absolute Truth inherently lacks any phenomenal qualities, how is it to be 'known'?[5]

About the sage or awakened being he says: 'The sage, by means of the *prajñā* which has no knowledge, illumines the Absolute Truth which has no phenomenal qualities.'[6] And in the following passage from the same text, the Emperor Wu, had he known his Sengzhao well enough, might have found a key to an understanding of Bodhidharma's strange behaviour if, that is, it can be 'understood' at all!

> Hence the sage is like an empty hollow. He cherishes no knowledge. He dwells in the world of change and utility, yet holds himself to the realm of non-activity (*wu wei*). He rests within the walls of the nameable, yet lives in the open country of what transcends speech. He is silent and alone, void and open, where his state of being cannot be clothed in language. Nothing more can be said of him.[7]

And for that matter, the doctrine of the suddenness of enlightenment, that came to be the hallmark of the most influential schools of Chan, was also already expounded in the early 5th century by Daosheng, another student of Kumārajīva. If, however, we comprehend the timelessness of the True Dharma, it should not surprise us that there have been parallels to and precursors of the central doctrines of Chan, not only in early Chinese Buddhism, but also in Daoism.

What is noteworthy, however, is that from the encounter and intermingling of Buddhism and Daoism in the course of a process of fermentation that took several centuries, the clear wine of Chan finally came matured. It proved to be a spirit that, to the present day, has intoxicated countless treasure hunters and was even responsible for the death of the ego of many of them due to an overdose of the True Dharma.

THE UNMISTAKABLE TASTE OF ZEN

It is fair to say that Zen is an offspring of the marriage of Buddhism and Daoism. With regard to Buddhism, the father, it is 'a chip off the old block' in so far as it is essentially all about the transmission of the Buddha Eye, the Treasury of the Eye of the True Dharma. With regard to Daoism, the mother (the Dao that so often is characterized as being female), it is equally a chip off the old block in its typically Chinese manner of expressing the enlightened view of all the patriarchs, and of mirroring the Inner Light.

The contribution of Daoism to this explosive mixture of Buddhism and Daoism, now well known as Zen Buddhism, is often underestimated. There have been many Buddhas (awakened beings) even before Shākyamuni Buddha, and even from outside Buddhism. But the fact that the combined explosive power of Buddhism and Daoism became such a deadly charge for blasting away all dualistic 'knowledge' that stands in the way of an unobstructed view of reality, is largely due to the 'detonator' that was contributed by Daoism and the Chinese mentality in general. This detonator is the peerless wit of the old Chan masters.

The paradoxical inner tension between seemingly irreconcilable opposites, that presses for a resolution in the liberating laughter of awakening, can be found in many statements by the Buddha, the Indian patriarchs and Buddhist scriptures. But in spite of the almost psychedelic colourfulness of the great Mahayana *sūtras*, Indian Buddhism has a strangely humourless dryness. One exception is that of the *mahāsiddhas* of Tantric Buddhism, a relatively late lineage of Buddhism that again emerged out of the intermingling of Buddhism with other elements, in this case Tantrism. A similar humourlessness (or less pejoratively, 'soberness') can also be found in 'Hindu' Zen, the Advaita Vedānta from Shankara to Ramana Maharshi.

The Chinese masters, however, who contributed the unmistakable Chinese flavour to Dhyāna Buddhism and thus created Chan, were masters of the punch line, of sparking off the Great Laughter that can manifest, as in the case of Mahākāshyapa, in a spontaneous smile but also as roaring, thigh-slapping laughter. It was their lunatic, absurd humour, their penchant for pranks and folly, that turned the rural farce of the Old Shākya into a knockabout comedy which seems absolutely outrageous to the worldview of the unenlightened, and makes Buster Keaton, Laurel and Hardy, and the Marx Brothers look like total amateurs of the genre.

Their historic patriarch, in this regard, was the old rascal Zhuangzi, who was, next to Laozi (also rather dry), the most important exponent of early Daoism. Zhuangzi's story about the Cloud General (as if one could give commands to the clouds!) and his encounter with Vast Obscurity – the embodiment of Daoist, and later Zen-Buddhist, 'not-knowing' – stands as a wonderful example of his shrewdness and hilarious wittiness:

Cloud General was wandering in the east when he passed by an offshoot of a whirlwind and happened to meet with Vast Obscurity. Vast Obscurity was just at that moment enjoying himself by slapping his thighs and hopping about like a sparrow. Seeing him, Cloud General came to a sudden halt and stood there reverentially. "Who are you, old man?" he asked. "Why are you doing this?"

"I'm playing," replied Vast Obscurity to Cloud General as he kept on slapping his thighs and hopping like a sparrow.

"I would like to ask you a question," said Cloud General.

"Pshaw!" said Vast Obscurity as he looked up and saw Cloud General.

"The vital breath of heaven is in disharmony," said Cloud General. "The vital breath of earth is in disarray. The six vital breaths of transformation are in discord. The four seasons are out of rhythm. Now I would like to blend the essence of the six vital breaths to foster all living beings. How shall I do this?"

"I don't know!" said Vast Obscurity as he

> turned his head away, continuing to slap his thighs and hop like a sparrow. "I don't know!"
>
> Cloud General was unable to ask any more questions. ...[8]

As in the case of the later Chan masters, Zhuangzi's craftiness consisted in guiding people to a comprehension of the Dao with what are, at the first glance, quite ordinary and innocent examples and stories that often reveal their depth only after diligent exploration and a long struggle to unlock the punch line, and *not* the 'moral of the tale'! 'I am going to talk to you about these things rather innocently,' he has one of his characters say to a treasure hunter, who had asked him for the highest meaning of holy truth, 'and you should listen to me rather innocently.'

And also the paradox, the conceptual hint at what is beyond thought (*para dokein*), plays a prominent role in Zhuangzi's work (as it does in the Mahayana *sūtras*). In the *Zhuangzi* we already find stories that resemble the later *gongan* (Jap. *kōan*) of the Zen masters with their interpenetration of paradox and absurd humour.

ZEN IN THE ART OF TELLING JOKES

There have been many attempts to describe and characterize the Zen training device called a *kōan*. Nothing could be further from the truth of what a *kōan* is than its characterization as a 'Zen riddle'. Even if the solution of a riddle may not be obvious at first glance, it nevertheless can be arrived at by logic and reason, as for example in the famous riddle of the Sphinx about the being that walks on four legs in the morning, on two legs at midday and on three legs in the evening.

The punch lines of the best jokes, however, suddenly unite two seemingly completely disparate things in a way that takes reason and the intellect by surprise and that cannot satisfactorily be explained by logic. That is why every joke immediately becomes stale when the punch line does not catch on spontaneously and one tries to *explain* it. The reaction to the punch line of a joke is not, as with the solution of a riddle, that which *can* be explained, an *intellectual* satisfaction, but an aesthetic delight in the unexpected and absurd association of two things that seemed to be formerly irreconcilable, and that becomes strikingly obvious all of a sudden, a delight that spontaneously explodes into laughter.

A monk asked master Yunmen:
"What is essential to the being of a patched-robe monk?"

The master replied: "Your turn!"

"Please, master, tell me!"

"Playing the zither for a cow."

Somebody asked master Yunmen: "How old are you, master?"

"Seven times nine makes sixty-eight."

"Why should seven times nine make sixty-eight?"

"On your behalf I have subtracted five years."

We can come close to the comprehension of *one* aspect of the Zen stories and *kōan* (as we will later see there are more aspects) if we take them to be a kind of joke. The Chinese masters of Chan have perfected the art of telling a joke in a genial and treacherous way, to a point which has not ever been surpassed. They tell us an absurd 'joke' which keeps us on tenterhooks for the punch line that would relieve the tension … and then they withhold the punch line from us in a most perfidious way. In this respect *kōan* are different from (for example) the humorous Sufi tales about the pranks of the crazy sage Mulla Nasruddin, which always supply the punch line like any conventional joke, even if they often reveal the full range of their meaning only after some contemplation.

The Chan masters leave it to *us* to find the punch line ourselves, a punch line in which the dualistic view of the world is transcended in a sudden leap to a non-dual level of comprehension. This punch line is 'consistent' in a way that cannot be figured out by logic and reason but that is existentially deeply satisfying and, to use a fashionable New Age expression, 'transformative', and it is so completely obvious, that 'afterwards' we strike our brow, perplexed about the incomprehensible fact that we did not 'get it' right away.

The inner struggle for the detonation of the punch line may take years. But it is worthwhile to get involved in the comedy of the Chan masters, since quite a few treasure hunters have, 'died with laughter' at their jokes, only to be reborn to the Great Life afterwards, blissfully smiling like a well-fed infant.

The monk Deng Yinfeng came to take leave of master Mazu. The master asked him where he was going, and Deng told him, he was going to see master Shitou.

Mazu said: "Shitou [lit.: the rock pinnacle] is slippery."

"I am equipped with a balancing pole, that I know how to make use of at all times," replied Deng Yinfeng.

When he reached his destination, he circumambulated the seat of Shitou once, shook his staff with the metal rings and asked: "What is this?"

Shitou cried: "Good heavens! Good heavens!"

Deng Yinfeng said nothing more, returned to Master Mazu and reported to him what had happened. Mazu charged him to return to Shitou. There, in case Shitou should shout 'Good heavens' again, he was to huff and hiss twice.

Deng Yinfeng went back to Shitou. He repeated, what he had done before, and again asked: "What is this?"

Thereupon Shitou huffed and hissed twice.

Again Deng Yinfeng departed without a further word.

He returned to master Mazu and reported, what had come to pass.

Mazu said: "Didn't I warn you right away that Shitou is slippery?"

From the *Jingde chuandenglu*, the 'Record of the Passing On of the Lamp, compiled in the Jingde era'

5

THE BARBARIAN FROM THE SOUTH

or

The Family Row about the Inheritance of Zen

*There are too many intellectuals in
this world*

*Who've studied far and wide and know
a lot of things.*

*But they don't know their own original
true nature*

And thus are wandering far from the Way.

Even if they explain reality in great detail

Of what avail are all those empty formulae?

*If in one instant you remember your
essential nature*

The Buddha's insight opens up to you.

Hanshan, 'Poems from Cold Mountain'

The repertory of the Chan masters would not have encompassed the full spectrum of the human and the all too human, had not their programme, as well as the comedy, also included the tragedy or, perhaps, the tragicomedy. The 33rd production of the drama of transmission did not disappoint us in this respect: the performance is of nearly Shakespearean scope, with all the facets from burlesque to the deepest existential conflict of 'to be or not to be', but nevertheless, with a happy ending that is not quite typical for Shakespeare's dramas. This play should prove to be as paradigmatic for the topic of 'succession' as is Shākyamuni's tale of the 'search'. That is to say, this story expresses patterns of human experience that have repeated themselves not only in Zen, but in all the other traditions of the 'transmission of the light', wherever they've occurred.

THE ENLIGHTENMENT OF AN ILLITERATE

Once again the protagonist of this play is a poor wretch, a chap who lived not only in material poverty, but who was also 'poor in spirit', but by no means lacking in spirit. His name is, Huineng, and his story is told in the so called 'Sūtra of the Sixth Patriarch, Spoken from the

Platform of the Dharma Treasury', also called the 'Sūtra of the Sixth Patriarch' or in short, the 'Platform Sūtra'. The 'platform' mentioned in the title was erected for the initiation of laypeople into the *buddhadharma*, and on this occasion the Sixth Patriarch 'preached' this *sūtra*. The importance of this text for Chinese Buddhism becomes evident when we realize that it is the only text of Chinese origin that was to be called a '*sūtra*', a designation that strictly speaking was reserved for texts that purported to transmit the teachings of Shākyamuni Buddha himself. As well as the essential teachings of Huineng, the Sixth Patriarch, it also contains an autobiography of this last official patriarch in the transmission lineage of Zen.

Let us have a look at the dramatic highlights of this most instructive play, without being put off by the probability (which seems to be confirmed by several historic sources) that it has not only condensed historic reality, but has also embellished and even, to a certain degree, 'corrected' it. What is of importance here is that, however it came to be written, this story expresses a kind of 'archetypal' reality which, if we get involved with it and come to grasp its punch lines, can unfold its transformative power in our heart-mind.

Once upon a time there was an illiterate young lad

called Huineng. His father, a learned government official from Fayang, had been removed from office and was exiled to Xinzhou in Lingnan, a province in the southern parts of China, reputed to be uncivilized. After the early death of his father Huineng lived with his mother, in extreme poverty, not far from Xinzhou in Nanhai, earning the rice for both of them by collecting and selling firewood. One day when he was delivering wood to the house of a customer, he overheard a stranger reciting the 'Diamond Sūtra' by the gate of the house:

> Thus have I heard. Upon a time Buddha sojourned in Anathapindika's Park by Shravasti with a great company of bhikshus [monks] even twelve hundred and fifty...
>
> Now in the midst of the assembly was the Venerable Subhuti. Forthwith he arose, uncovered his right shoulder, knelt upon his right knee, and, respectfully raising his hands with palms joined, addressed the Buddha thus:
>
> World-honoured One, if good men and good women seek the Consummation of Incomparable Enlightenment, by what criteria should they abide and how should they control their thoughts? ... [9]

Huineng paused to listen to the recitation. And further on he heard sentences like:

> Therefore, Subhuti, all Bodhisattvas, lesser and great, should develop a pure, lucid mind, not depending upon sound, flavour, touch, odour or any quality. A Bodhisattva should develop a mind which alights upon no thing whatsoever; and so should he establish it.[10]

In his autobiography Huineng reports: 'I heard it only once. And my mind opened up and cleared.'

What the Sixth Patriarch unspectacularly called an 'opening and clearing' of his mind, must, as soon will become evident, have been an enlightenment experience of considerable depth. He suddenly found himself in the 'vast emptiness' of the Eye of the True Dharma, in the cool and clear openness and loneliness of total subjectivity for which there are no 'objects' any more that the mind could 'alight upon'. And so, as it happened to many others who found themselves in a similar situation, a longing must have stirred in him to find some kind of confirmation of the validity of this experience that, according to all standards of the prevalent 'common sense', seemed so insane.

Diamond Sūtra (Skrt. *Vajracchedikā-prajñāpāramitā-sūtra*, the 'Sūtra of the Diamond Cutter of Transcendent Wisdom') is an independent part of the 'Sūtra of Transcendent Wisdom'. It shows that phenomena are not the absolute reality but illusions, projections of one's own mind. Thus the meditator should recognize them as empty, devoid of any substance, and should not abide with phenomenal appearances.

The wisdom that recognizes this emptiness is called the 'Diamond Cutter' since it is 'indestructible' and sharp as a diamond, which cuts off all arbitrary concepts and thus leads the practitioner to the 'further shore' of enlightenment.

Thus Huineng inquired of the man who had been reciting, from where he had brought that *sūtra*. As he reports in the 'Platform Sūtra':

> He answered: "I have made obeisance to the Fifth Patriarch, Hung-jen [Hongren], at the East Mountain, Fengmu shan ... At present there are over a thousand disciples there.

> While I was there I heard the Master encourage the monks and lay followers, saying that if they recited just the one volume, the Diamond Sūtra, they could see into their own natures and with direct apprehension become Buddhas."[11]

Hearing this, Huineng realized that he had been predestined to hear this text. A generous donation he received from a benefactor allowed him to provide for his mother, and thus he took leave of her and wandered off to northern China to pay his respect to Hongren, the Fifth Patriarch, on Mount Fengmu. Hongren was said to be a man who had come to know the enlightening power of the 'Diamond Sūtra' and who had himself realized the insights contained therein. Now Huineng wanted to check out this man and his realization – and in doing so his own realization at the same time. He wanted to have it examined, confirmed and deepened.

FATHER AND SON SING WITH ONE MOUTH

We must not forget that we are in the China of the 7th century CE, without cars or public transport, with rough paths through the wilderness on which not only wild animals, but also robbers and highwaymen were lying in wait for the traveller. After a long, and probably arduous, walk, Huineng arrived at Mount Fengmu, and the monastery of the Fifth Patriarch. According to the Platform Sūtra the following dialogue occurred when he went to see Hongren:

> The master asked me: "Where are you from that you come to this mountain to make obeisance to me? Why do you come to me? What are you looking for?"
>
> I replied: "I am a commoner from Xinzhou in Lingnan. I have come from far away only to make obeisance to the Master. I am seeking no particular thing; I seek only to become a Buddha."
>
> The master said: "If you are from Lingnan then you are a barbarian. How could you become a Buddha?"

> I replied: "People may be from the south or from the north, but in buddha-nature there originally is no south and north. The social status of this barbarian may be different from the social status of the Master, but the buddha-nature is just the same, there is no difference."

Now obviously this is not only a typical *wenda* ('question and answer', Jap. *mondō*) between a treasure hunter and a Chan master, but also what later would be called a 'dharma contest'; an exchange between two enlightened people who, playfully, as in foil fencing between friends, test their mutual talent for repartee. Just by the body language and the whole comportment of a person who comes to see him or her, a Zen master is already able to recognize the state of mind of this person. Thus, Hongren certainly was aware already that his visitor was an outstanding person, even before Huineng opened his mouth.

Therefore, Hongren begins right away to challenge and test him, seemingly quite innocently (with best regards from Zhuangzi) about his comings and goings. And Huineng answers with equal innocence, and apparently from the perspective of a naïve commoner from the south, 'Well, I'm coming from this and that place and, if you don't mind, I just want to become a Buddha' – not more, not less. As if he did not already know better! But maybe now it is his turn to test Hongren.

Hongren plays along with him and apparently answers from the point of view of an unenlightened mind, at the same time throwing him the bait, tempting him to show his shark's teeth: 'A Buddha is something so lofty and sublime – how could an uneducated commoner from the south hope ever to become a Buddha?' As if he didn't know better!

Huineng takes the bait and is thrashing about on Hongren's hook, and with his answer he is showing his true face with the already blinking dharma eye. Huineng further reports: 'Even though the Master wanted to continue our exchange, when he saw that other disciples were nearby, he sent me off to work with them.' Hongren has seen enough; he is well aware that the comprehension of this young layman already surpasses that of most of the monks in his monastery who have been his disciples for a long time. And one who sees with the dharma eye certainly is longing to encounter like-minded people. So it is quite understandable that Hongren would have *loved* to go on playfully fencing with Huineng and to 'continue their exchange'. But he also was well aware how easily envy, jealousy and malevolence overwhelm all pious aspirations in the human heart. Had he shown his appreciation of this shabby barbarian too obviously, and had he dedicated more time to him than to the other disciples, this might have triggered poisonous rivalry. He did not want to run this risk, but wanted to protect this precious young sprout so that it could grow unnoticed and undisturbed.

In a dharma contest the two fencers know quite well, and without a referee calling out 'touché', when a blow has found its mark. So Hongren does not address the issue of Huineng's response with any further remark. He treats him like any old Tom, Dick or Harry among his monks and sends him off to work. Huineng, however, in his elation about his own fencing art and his recent enlightenment experience thinks that he has to top it off. He recounts:

> I said to him: "My own mind, not being separated from my own essential nature, always produces wisdom. This in itself is a field of virtue. What other work does the Master require me to do?"

Wisely spoken, indeed. But Hongren knows the elation of a fresh breakthrough, and puts a damper on this youthful hothead so that Huineng, as inconspicuously as possible, and out of the line of fire from jealous monks, may go on simmering in his own juice and become, 'well done'. So Hongren retorted: "This barbarian is very sharp! You had better shut your mouth and retire to the back yard of the monastery to work in the rice mill."

THE MIRROR THAT CANNOT BE POLISHED CLEAN

Huineng toddled off to work. In one of the back yards of the big monastery compound (as we have heard, around 1,000 disciples had gathered around Hongren on Mount Fengmu) he chopped wood and pedalled the rice mill for many months without calling on the Fifth Patriarch again. Hongren and Huineng had 'seen' each other, and that was enough. Hongren had told Huineng to go to work, and that is what he did. Chopping wood for him was not inferior to working in one of the higher positions in the monastery. And that Huineng did not seek out Hongren again, even though the latter had not confirmed his enlightenment with one single word, just shows how sure he was of himself, and how firmly established he was in his experience. After eight months Huineng finally received a sign from Hongren. One day the master unexpectedly showed up in the shed where Huineng was working:

> Then suddenly the Fifth Patriarch came and said: "I know that your insight is authentic; that is why I was afraid, people might do you harm. That is why I did not talk to you any longer. Did you understand?"
>
> I said: "I understood your intention, and this is why I did not come forward to your room so that people would not know."

And so Huineng continued to chop wood, but the 'Sūtra of the Sixth Patriarch' does not say for how long. Then one day the Fifth Patriarch saw his end drawing near and he wanted to take care of his succession. Of course he knew who he was dealing with and who in his monastery would be worthy of receiving the robe that had been handed on for generations as a sign of the transmission of the patriarchy. But this still had to be demonstrated in an obvious manner to all the disciples in his monastery. This is why he staged a drama that would reveal the state of consciousness of all the protagonists in this new version of the play of transmission. He called his disciples together, and when they had assembled he first reminded them that 'the question of life and death is of vital importance' and reproached them for only seeking good karma for their next incarnation by performing external religious rituals, and for not really aiming to 'escape the bitter sea of birth and death'. Bodhidharma had done much the same thing by warning the Emperor Wu of Liang that his pious activities would, in the end, bring him 'no merit'.

And then, the Fifth Patriarch challenged them:

> All of you, return to your rooms and look into yourselves. Men of wisdom will of themselves grasp the original nature of their *prajñā* intuition. Each of you write a verse and bring it to me. I will read your verses, and if there is one who is awakened to the cardinal meaning, I will give him the robe and the dharma and make him the sixth patriarch. Hurry, hurry! [12]

If Hongren urges his monks to 'hurry, hurry', it is not because he himself is in such a hurry, but because he knows that the '*prajñā* intuition' occurs instantly and spontaneously (as in the case of Huineng hearing the Diamond Sūtra only once) and that no amount of

Prajñā**,** lit. 'wisdom', in the Mahayana school of Buddhism, and thus also in Zen, denotes the Supreme Wisdom or 'Transcendent Wisdom' (*prajñāpāramitā*), the wisdom that reaches the 'other shore' of enlightenment. Thus, as Sengzhao stated, '*prajñā* is not knowledge', it is not philosophical understanding arrived at through discursive thinking, but a wisdom that manifests as a direct intuitive comprehension of the true nature of things. A decisive aspect of this kind of wisdom is the comprehension that emptiness (insubstantiality) is the ultimate nature of the world.

The realization and actualization of *prajñā* in Zen is equated with enlightenment and is regarded as one of the essential hallmarks of Buddhahood.

cogitation and pondering will lead the monks to 'grasp their original nature'. But the monks, stuck in the rut of their pious practices, their learning and their discursive thinking, do just that, they start to think about what would be the 'right' thing for them to do now.

Now among the disciples of Hongren there was a monk named Shenxiu who, for a long time, had held the position of the Eldest in the monastery. He was known to all of the other disciples as Hongren's 'right hand'. Shenxiu was well versed in the holy scriptures like the 'Diamond Sūtra' that was praised by the Fifth Patriarch; he knew how to lead the monks in their daily monastic ceremonies and he had practised *zazen* for such a long time that he was able to instruct others in theory and practice of the way of Zen. Nevertheless, as Hongren was well aware, Shenxiu had not yet 'entered the gate and realized his own True Nature'. The other disciples, however, themselves lacking in the Eye of the True Dharma, assessed Shenxiu only according to the outer appearance of his position in the monastery and therefore assumed without questioning that his insight surpassed their own: 'The monk Shenxiu is our teacher. Certainly he will obtain the robe and the dharma.' And so they did not even consider writing a verse on their own.

Thus all the monks were looking at Shenxiu, and he knew that everybody expected him to demonstrate his enlightened comprehension by writing the proper verse. But in contrast to Huineng, who had not even been ordained as a monk and who was working as a layman for the kitchen of the monastery without hankering for any higher position, Shenxiu was not that sure of himself and of the soundness of his Zen experience. Several times he got as far as the front of the lecture hall with the intention to present the verse he had composed, but each time he shrunk back, breaking out in a cold sweat. Therefore, the thought occurred to him to make his verse public, but anonymously: 'It might be best for me to write my verse on the wall of the corridor (in front of the room of the Master) where the Master can see it. When he says that it is good, I will come forth with a bow and declare that the composition is mine.' So holding a candle in one hand he wrote his verse on the wall in the middle of the night. The verse said:

The body is the bodhi tree,
The mind is like a clear mirror on its stand.
We must diligently polish it at all times,
Not letting any dust gather on it.

Then he returned to his room, not finding any sleep for the rest of the night, torn between hope and fear: hope for the acknowledgement and confirmation by the Fifth Patriarch, fear that his insight could be weighed and found wanting so that he would not 'obtain the dharma'. When Hongren saw the verse next morning, the cunning old devil called all his disciples together, burned incense in front of the writing on the wall and admonished all the monks to memorize the verse and to recite it regularly from then on: "Whoever practises according to this verse will avoid falling into the three evil paths." [Hell, hungry ghosts and beasts].

So far, so good, but between 'not falling into evil paths' and realizing the 'Treasury of the Eye of the True Dharma' there obviously is a slight difference. Just as Zen masters often hide praise in a seeming reproach, the Fifth Patriarch, for all who have ears to hear, now voices a reproach in the form of seeming praise. Mirroring Shenxiu's state of mind, Hongren's reaction addresses the same level of understanding as Shenxiu's verse: that of the phenomenal world, of cause and effect, of virtuous deeds and their karmic retributions. But as their paralyzing reverence for their 'teacher', Shenxiu, has already shown, the other monks and disciples did *not* have eyes and ears: 'All the disciples recited the verse and cried out in admiration: "How excellent!"' Alas, not without good reason, Buddha Shākyamuni himself had already admonished his disciples in his discourse to the Kalamas that none of them should accept the teachings of a teacher just because that teacher possessed a high rank and good reputation without having verified their truth by their own direct experience. The 'Platform Sūtra' further reports:

> At midnight the Fifth Patriarch called Shenxiu to his room and said: "Did you write this verse? If you wrote it, one should suppose that you have grasped the core of my teaching."

Another bit of skilful dodging by Hongren. He has seen through Shenxiu's scheming and is luring him out of his hiding with this ambiguous 'one should suppose'. And, of course, Shenxiu swallows the bait and humbly confesses to be the author of the much praised verse: "I beg the Master in his compassion to tell me whether he sees even a little bit of wisdom and discernment in my mind." Well, the Master saw into his mind, indeed, and what he saw was that Shenxiu's verse not only expresses a dualistic point of view that presupposes a distinction between body and mind, but that it also propagates an 'orthodox' Buddhist understanding of the path to enlightenment. According to this understanding it is necessary, gradually, to purify the mind of all impurities by constant practice in order, eventually, to 'become' a Buddha.

Certainly, Hongren did not intend to negate that constant meditative practice which rids and purifies the mind of all concepts is the basis of the way of Zen, otherwise he would not have encouraged the monks to learn Shenxiu's verse by heart and to practise accordingly.

But at the same time he was aware that from the point of view of the '*prajñā* nature of the original mind' one cannot *become* a Buddha by practice. And he not only saw that this *prajñā* mind was lacking in Shenxiu's verse, but he also had the boundless compassion not to confirm, for 'political' reasons, a person as dharma successor who was not yet really qualified as such. The Zen tradition holds that a dharma heir must *surpass* his master in order for the lineage not to degenerate, and he did not take lightly his responsibility that far exceeded the continued existence of a monastery of a thousand inhabitants, even though (or rather just because) his compassion embraced every one of them. Had he entrusted the patriarchy to Shenxiu he would not only have cheated hundreds of disciples, but also Shenxiu himself, out of the incentive, eventually, to realize their own *prajñā* mind, and thus become true heirs to the treasure he himself had inherited from a long lineage of patriarchs.

This is why, now that they are in private and Shenxiu will not be embarrassed in front of the other monks, he does not mince his words and he tells Shenxiu that he has not yet seen his original nature, and that ultimate enlightenment cannot be realized by the method of gradual progress that his verse propagates. In his grandfatherly compassion, he not only points out to him, with an eloquence rather atypical for later Chan masters, what ultimate enlightenment is all about, outlining the teaching of 'sudden enlightenment' that had always been the hallmark of the Zen tradition, but he also gives him a second chance:

> Ultimate enlightenment requires you to grasp your original mind directly, and in one moment, to realize that your own nature is originally without birth and death, and to comprehend anytime and everywhere with every thought that the myriad things [all phenomena] never stand still. It means to comprehend that one truth is the whole truth and that every thing in its true nature incorporates the whole truth; that the mind in its suchness *is* the truth. To comprehend in this way is the inherent nature of ultimate enlightenment. Go back (to your room) now and contemplate this for a day or two. Then compose another verse and bring it to me. If I see from this verse that you have entered the gate and have realized your own original nature, I will hand over the robe and the dharma to you.

Shenxiu did as Hongren had told him, but even after several days of contemplating the words of the Fifth Patriarch he did not arrive at grasping the depth of their meaning and accordingly write a new verse. Here again we see very clearly that the dharma, just like the Dao, cannot be 'given' to anybody. Even if Hongren's words were unmistakably clear and to the point, a mere intellectual 'understanding' of them was not sufficient to make Shenxiu really grasp their truth. What Hongren meant by 'handing over' would just have been a formal confirmation of Shenxiu's awakening to his own original nature by himself. But this did not come to pass and so 'his mind was perturbed and he did not find any rest. It was like a bad dream and everything he did felt uneasy and joyless.'

A few days later a lay brother, who was reciting Shenxiu's verse, passed by the shack where Huineng was working. Huineng heard the verse, and knew instantly that the author of this verse had not yet grasped the fundamental essence, his true nature. So he inquired from the lay brother why he was reciting this verse, and thus heard for the first time about Hongren's challenge, and also what the Fifth Patriarch had said about Shenxiu's verse. He asked the lay brother to take him to where the verse was, in the corridor, so that he could pay respects to it. There, he encountered a vice-governor who was just passing by, and asked him to read the verse aloud for him since he was illiterate himself:

> "He read the verse aloud and I comprehended its meaning. Thus I said to the vice-governor: 'I have a verse too; please write it on the wall for me!'
>
> "The vice-governor said: 'How can it be that a barbarian like you would compose a verse. This is really extraordinary.'"

The vice-governor was not the only one to be amazed. Up to our present day many learned commentators of the 'Sūtra of the Sixth Patriarch' just could not believe that an illiterate should be able to comprehend the highest wisdom. Maybe because they themselves have no direct experience of the fundamental difference of intellectual discursive *knowledge* and direct intuitive *wisdom* (*prajñā*), they have suspected that the emphasis on Huineng's illiteracy was just a clever literary trick to stress the fact that Zen is not about book learning and intellectual brilliance, but that the Sixth Patriarch nevertheless … If, however, Huineng's father really had died early and had left his wife and his young son in bitter poverty, it is quite probable that Huineng had no literary education at all, since in his day and age this was a privilege of the rich upper class. Even later, when Huineng already was a widely respected master of the *buddhadharma*, he needed to ask one of his students who had some questions on the 'Lotus Sūtra', to read the text out loud for him, before he could instruct him on its deep meaning which, on hearing it, he grasped instantly through his *prajñā*. (*See* the 'Platform Sūtra', chapter 37)

Now the verse that the 'barbarian from the south' composed was:

For bodhi there really is no tree
Nor any mirror on a stand.
Originally there is not a single thing,
So where could dust be gathering?

When this was written down, Huineng returned to his shack and resumed his work threshing rice. All the monks who read the verse were not only amazed by it, but also full of admiration and praise for a man whom, until now, they had mistakenly taken, as they now realized, to be a barbarian. But the Fifth Patriarch, who saw that jealousy was already stirring among them, was concerned about his young protégé. Thus, to derail their malevolence he said:

"This verse does not yet express the highest truth. Why should one admire it?" And immediately all the monks conceded that the verse really was not *that* good, and went on with their monkish business.

As he had already done with his remarks on Shenxiu's verse, Hongren, the crafty old rascal, had again achieved his goal to preserve peace in the monastery without telling a lie. Yes, *why* should one admire this verse? Had the monks only really penetrated to this point? As the contemporary Japanese Zen master Soko Morinaga Rōshi says in his commentary on the 'Platform Sūtra', this verse indeed does not *explicitly* express the *prajñā* mind that 'recognizes one's own mind and the myriad things as one'. However, as Morinaga Rōshi says:

> And yet this meaning is definitely expressed in the line: "Originally there is not a (single) thing.' This 'no thing', a synonym for emptiness, designates equality or, in other words, the non-existence of any distinctness of self and others. To think that no dust could be gathering, because there is nothing that it could gather on, is wrong since this emptiness is not just a nihilistic nothing, but *is* the

> myriad things. Everything in its suchness is the appearance of this emptiness, and only since everything is the manifestation of this emptiness, there is nothing on which dust could be gathering.[13]

Hongren had of course recognized the *prajñā* mind in Huineng's verse. That is why the next day he showed up in the shack where Huineng was working and indicated to him in a covert manner that he should come to his room secretly in the middle of the night. There he once again tested and confirmed Huineng's Zen eye and handed over the robe and the bowl (the begging bowl that is one of the few possessions of a Buddhist monk) as a symbol of the transmission of the patriarchy to him.

Knowing the human heart well enough, the Fifth Patriarch was quite aware that the transmission of the dharma to this barbarian would meet with strong resistance among his long-standing disciples, especially with Shenxiu, and could trigger violent reactions among the others. Thus he said to Huineng: "All along the life of those who have transmitted the dharma has been hanging on a thin thread. If you stay here, some people might do you harm. You should leave at once." He further advised him to return to the south and to stay in

Student or disciple? – Even though the word 'disciple' may sound a bit antiquated to some readers, the expressions 'master and disciple' are given preference in this book over 'teacher and student', since the latter seems to suggest that Zen can be 'taught' and 'studied' like any academic subject matter. But what is transmitted from heart-mind to heart-mind in this special relationship between someone who has mastered *himself*, and someone who disciplines *himself* under the guidance of a master, is not objectified knowledge that can be taught and studied like, for example, mathematics. The great Chan master, Huangbo, also hints at this distinction in the 11th case of the *Biyanlu* (even though this *kōan* still has a much deeper meaning):

> Huangbo once addressed the assembly and said: "You are, all of you, a bunch of dreg-lickers. If you are on pilgrimage all of the time, where will you have your Today? Don't you know that in all of China there are no Chan teachers?"
>
> A monk came forward and asked: "But surely there are those in various places who accept disciples and preside over assemblies. What about that?"
>
> Huangbo replied: "I did not say there is no Chan, only there are no Chan teachers."

hiding without teaching for five years. Then he accompanied Huineng down the mountain and personally ferried him across the river. He himself, so he confided to Huineng, would leave the world one year[14] later, and this is exactly as it came to pass.

THE HERITAGE THAT CANNOT BE SNATCHED AWAY

After he had returned to his monastery the Fifth Patriarch did not give any discourses on the dharma for several days in a row. When the monks eventually asked him for the reason, he answered: "I am not ill, but the robe of Bodhidharma already went away to the south." Interestingly enough, he speaks about the 'robe' that 'went away' (a robe with legs?) and not about the person who carried it, or the dharma. From the point of view of his dharma eye, the robe is not a symbol for the dharma, and Huineng is not a carrier of the dharma, but the robe *is* the dharma *is* Huineng. Did he not instruct Shenxiu only a short time ago that enlightenment 'means to comprehend that … every thing in its true nature incorporates the whole truth'?

When his disciples heard that the patriarchy had been transmitted, and concluded from the absence of the barbarian from the south that he had taken it away with him, things just came to pass as Hongren had predicted. His long-standing disciples were not pleased at all to hear that the patriarchy had been conferred to an illiterate bum from the south, and several hundreds of them set out to persecute Huineng to 'snatch away the robe and the dharma from him'. However, Hongren's delaying tactics had given Huineng a lead of several days over his persecutors, and so most of them gave up on the way (even now their desire for the dharma was not strong enough to overcome their indolence) – well, almost all of them. A former army general, a 'coarse and violent character' by the name of Zheng Huiming, finally caught up with the Sixth Patriarch after two months when Huineng had just reached Mount Dayu. The Sixth Patriarch reports:

> On the mountaintop he caught up with me. Thus I put down the robe on a rock and said: "This robe represents our faith. It cannot be taken by force and violence." Then I hid in the bushes.
>
> Huiming approached the robe and wanted to lift it up, but it did not move. Then he called out to me: "I have come after you for the

> dharma, not to snatch the robe away
> from you."

Thereupon Huineng came from his hiding and immediately began to instruct Huiming on the dharma, saying, "Since you have come for the dharma, you should shut out all objects and not let a single thought arise." Huiming remained in silence for a long while, and then the Sixth Patriarch asked him, "When you think neither 'good' nor 'bad' – what is your original face right now?" On hearing this, Huiming was suddenly enlightened. The question about the 'original face', and the challenge to demonstrate the response 'right now', without recourse to discursive thinking and dualistic concepts has been raised ever since in encounters between Zen masters and their disciples.

THE CORE OF THE TEACHINGS OF THE SIXTH PATRIARCH

The story of the Sixth Patriarch up to this point has been recounted here at such great length because the 'Sūtra of the Sixth Patriarch' is so full of spiritual treasures, one feels tempted to quote the whole text. Fortunately there exist good English translations of the 'Platform Sūtra', all varying in minor details of this story, based as they are on different Chinese versions of the *Liuzu dashi fabao tanjing*. They nevertheless agree in the essential points of the autobiography of Huineng and his later teachings. It is worthwhile to read them, since the Huineng act in the ongoing rural farce about the transmission of the light, is of central importance to the whole of the history of Zen. For even if the process of the maturing of the wine of Chan took, as we have already pointed out, several centuries, we may regard Huineng as the master who marks the beginning of Chan in its typical expression of a Dhyāna Buddhism, which has been completely assimilated by the Chinese mentality.

With Huineng, we find the 'teaching of sudden enlightenment' in one of its clearest forms, while Huineng stresses at the same time, "But he who grasps the original mind himself, and sees his essential nature, knows that (this) distinction does not exist. This is why 'sudden' and 'gradual' are only provisional concepts." And ever since Huineng, Chan has departed even more radically than before from the orthodox teachings of Mahayana Buddhism, as expounded in the *Lankāvatāra-sūtra* that was propagated by Bodhidharma, or the *Vajracchedikā-prajñnpāramitā-sūtra* ('Diamond Sūtra') that was praised by the Fifth Patriarch, in order to develop a typically Chinese form of instruction.

To round up the story of the Sixth Patriarch, we have to add that after five years of living in seclusion he finally showed up in Canton, where he disclosed his identity as the Sixth Patriarch of Chan to the dharma master Yinzhong, the abbot of the Faxing monastery. Yinzhong ordained Huineng, who until now had been a layman, as a monk, and then asked him to accept him as his first disciple. This is how the teaching career of the Sixth Patriarch began, and it would continue for more than 40 years until his death in 713CE. At his first encounter with Yinzhong, Huineng immediately indicated the basic principle that would both characterize and drive his teaching method 'outside orthodox teaching'.

Yinzhong asked: "When the Fifth Patriarch transmitted the dharma to you, what did he teach you? What did he transmit to you?"

I replied: "There is nothing that was taught, nothing that was transmitted. It was just a matter of seeing one's own nature. Meditation and liberation [and other 'Buddhist' questions] were not discussed."

Yinzhong asked: "Why were meditation and liberation not discussed?"

I said: "Because this would have been a consideration of opposites and not Buddhism. Buddhism is the teaching of nonduality."

Good friends, in this teaching of mine, from ancient times up to the present, all have set up no-thought as the main doctrine, non-form as the substance, and non-abiding as the basis. Non-form is to be separated from form even when associated with form. No-thought is not to think even when involved in thought. Non-abiding is the original nature of man.

Successive thoughts do not stop; prior thoughts, present thoughts and future thoughts follow one after the other without cessation. If one instant of thought is cut off, the dharma body separates from the physical body, and in the midst of successive thoughts there will be no place for attachment to anything. If one instant of thought clings, then successive thoughts cling; this is known as being fettered. If in all things successive thoughts do not cling, then you are unfettered. Therefore, non-abiding is made the basis.

Huineng in the *Liuzu dashi fabao tanjing*
(translated by Philip B Yampolsky)

6

STICK AND SHOUT

or

How to Teach the Unteachable

Once when the great master Mazu was out walking with Baizhang, they saw some wild ducks flying by.

The great master said: "What is this?"

Baizhang said: "Wild ducks."

Mazu said: "Where have they flown to?"

Baizhang said: "They flew away."

Thereupon the great master pinched Baizhang's nose.

Baizhang cried out in pain. The great master said: "How could they have flown away?"

Hearing these words Baizhang had insight.

From the *Jingde chuandenglu*

HUINENG AS THE 'FATHER' OF CHAN

With Huineng, the sixth Chinese patriarch, Dhyāna Buddhism had not only taken root in China but was beginning to bring forth typically Chinese fruit. The early masters of Chan were either still strongly influenced by the Indian Mahayana Buddhism and its doctrines and scriptures, or they were, like Sengcan, the third Chinese patriarch, (and author of the *Xinxinming*) so deeply rooted in Daoism that their teaching was a virtual restatement of the + in Daoist terminology.

The special flavour of Chan was already recognizable to a certain extent in Bodhidharma and the words and deeds of the Chinese masters of early Channa. However, the unmistakable form of spiritual training that is known today as Chan or Zen was only beginning to crystallize during the days of the Sixth Patriarch. And even though it was not Huineng alone who single-handedly gave Channa its Chinese form of expression, he certainly was the most influential figure of early Chan, and is thus considered the father of Chan proper.

This does not mean that more orthodox flavoured forms of Chinese Dhyāna Buddhism abruptly disappeared with Huineng. The so-called Northern School of

Chan, which was established by Shenxiu after Huineng's departure to the south, was promoted by the court; it flourished for a short time and produced a number of noticeable Buddhist teachers. And even Huineng, in his 'Platform Sūtra', often refers to the Mahayana *sūtras*, but then continues to expound them in a rather unorthodox way. The lineage of learned dharma teachers in the succession of Shenxiu, however, died out within a few generations, while the lineage established by Huineng the 'illiterate', the tradition that later on would be called the 'Zen of the Patriarchs', continued to flourish and spread. Obviously the widest knowledge of Buddhist doctrines, all eagerness to 'wipe the mirror clean', and protection by the high and mighty, were not sufficient to keep alive a form of the 'School of Enlightenment' that lacked the inner spark, the spark that Hongren already missed in Shenxiu, his well known and widely respected close disciple. This spark is the 'ultimate enlightenment' Hongren talked about, or what in later Chan (which increasingly avoided using abstract terms such as 'enlightenment') was called the direct apprehension of one's original face.

By the end of the 8th and the beginning of the 9th century, after a few more stagings of the rural farce of the 'Transmission of the Light', practically all prominent actors on the stage of Chan belonged to the Southern School of Huineng. And since Huineng had abstained from officially passing on the patriarchy by bestowing Bodhidharma's robe to one single disciple, and had confirmed several of his disciples as heirs of his dharma, the Chan of the Southern School started to spread over China like wildfire. During the coming two centuries, which marked the 'Golden Age' of Zen, an apogee of the Zen spirit unequalled until today, China produced a virtually unbelievable abundance of outstanding Zen masters.

THE SHOCK TREATMENT OF PATRIARCH MA

Not long after Huineng, however, a downright scandalous demoralization spread among the leading protagonists of Chan. In view of the boorishness that started to take hold on the Chan scene, many an upright Buddhist might wonder what *this* was supposed to have in common with the lofty doctrine of Gautama Buddha. And, of course, once again it was a chap with a rather barbarian attitude who was at the bottom of the scandal. If we hear what the ancient sources report about his appearance, we might think that Bodhidharma, the

Barbarian from the West, had reappeared. The *Chuandenglu* says, 'He was of striking appearance and impressive manner. He had the piercing gaze of a tiger and walked ambling like a cow. He could touch the tip of his nose with his tongue, and on the soles of his feet there were marks in the shape of a wheel.'

Striking indeed, if not outright scary, Jiangxi Daoyi (709–88) would go down in the annals of Zen as Mazu, 'The Patriarch (from the House of) Ma'. He is considered the greatest master of Chan after Huineng, which is also reflected by the fact that he is the only master after Huineng who is traditionally called a 'patriarch'. In the incident with Baizhang and the ducks, quoted at the beginning of this chapter, we already get a taster of how this Mazu taught his disciples about what is what. That this ruffian demeanour was not just an unfortunate slip by an otherwise dignified Buddhist master, but that there was method in this madness, is documented by a number of other reports on the scandalous behaviour of Patriarch Ma:

> A monk asked: "What is the meaning of Bodhidharma's coming from the West?"
>
> The Master beat him and said: "If I would not beat you, people all over the country would laugh at me."

The monk Shuiliao came to see the master and asked him, "What is the meaning of Bodhidharma's coming from the West?"

Mazu did not answer but insinuated that Shuiliao bow down and retire. When Shuiliao was about to prostrate himself, Mazu kicked him so hard he fell on the floor. At the same moment Shuiliao experienced enlightenment.

Clapping his hands and laughing out loud, Shuiliao got up and said: "Wonder of wonders! A hundred thousand *samādhis* [meditative absorptions] and countless spiritual insights have their root and source in the tip of a hair!" Then he prostrated once again before Mazu and left.

When Shuiliao had become abbot of a monastery himself, he often said to his monks: "Ever since I received this kick by Mazu, I have not stopped laughing."

Once when his disciple Baizhang approached him, Mazu reached for the flywhisk lying next to his seat, and raised it into the air.

> Baizhang asked: "Right this moment when you are doing this, should you not be free of being attached to doing so?"
>
> Mazu returned the flywhisk to its place. For a moment Baizhang was dumbfounded.
>
> Mazu said: "You may open your mouth and go on jabbering. But how will you manage to come to enlightenment?"
>
> Baizhang reached for the flywhisk and raised it into the air.
>
> Mazu asked: "Right at this moment when you are doing this, should you not be free of being attached to doing so?"
>
> When Baizhang leaned forward to return the flywhisk to its place, Mazu shouted, "Ho!" into his ear so loudly, that Baizhang was deaf for three days.

It is said that Baizhang realized complete enlightenment when being hit by this shout.

Nose-twistings, bashings, kicks and deafening shouts, Mazu, this much-venerated offspring of Bodhidharma, seems to have been quite a rascal. These stories make Mazu look more like a juvenile hooligan then like a dignified exponent of the *buddhadharma*. With his noxious influence on his contemporaries and dharma heirs, Mazu turned the rural farce of the Old Shākya literally into a slapstick comedy. His example set a precedent, and in a little while many of the great Chinese Chan masters took to beating, kicking and shouting without shame.

The Five Houses of Zen

By transmitting the Treasury of the Eye of the True Dharma in their own idiosyncratic way, prominent heirs of Huineng's Zen of the Patriarchs founded the five major schools of Chan in China, the so called 'Five Houses'.

1. The Guiyang School (Jap. Igyō School) named after the first characters of the names of the two founders, Guishan Lingyou (Isan Reiyū, 771–853, a dharma grandson of Mazu Daoyi) and his disciple Yangshan Huiji (Kyōzan Ejaku, 807–83). The hallmark of the Guiyang School was its use of a system of 97 symbols inscribed in a circle, which made up a kind of secret code for communication among people with deep Zen experience. The system has been lost, and the tradition of the Guiyang School later on merged with the Linji School.

2. The Linji School (Jap. Rinzai School) founded by Linji Yixuan (Rinzai Gigen, died 867) who is

a dharma heir of Mazu Daoi (Baso Dōitsu, 709–88) via Huangbo Xiyun (Ōbaku Kiun, 720–814) and Baizhang Huaihai (Hyakujō Ekai, 720–814) and who perfected Mazu's unusual methods of instruction. Later on the Linji School was mainly related to *kōan* practice. Myōan Eisai (1141–1215) and Nampo Jōmyō (1235–1309) brought the Linji School to Japan, where it remains active today, the Rinzai School. The Korean Chogye School of Zen also is rooted in the Linji lineage and was founded by Taego Pou (1301–81).

3. The Caodong School (Jap. Sōtō School) named after the first characters of the names of the two founders, Caoshan Benji (Sōzan Honjaku, 840–901) and his master Dongshan Liangjie (Tōzan Ryōkai, 807–69). The lineage of the Caodong School goes back to Shitou Xiqian (Sekitō Kisen, 700–90) who was, after Huineng and next to Mazu Daoyi, one of the most influential masters during the formative years of Chan. While Linji Zen emphasized the striving

for awakening through the 'contemplation of words' (*kōan* practice) the emphasis in Caodong Zen is on 'silent illumination', the mere sitting in meditative absorption (Jap. *shikantaza*) without any intent. The Caodong School was brought to Japan by Eihei Dōgen (also Dōgen Zenji, 1200–53) and is, today, the second major school active there.

4. The Yunmen School (Jap. Ummon School), founded by Yunmen Wenyan (Ummon Bun'en, 864–949), which also goes back to Shitou Xiqian via great masters like Xuefeng Yitsun (Seppō Gison, 822–908) and Deshan Xuanjian (Tokusan Senkan, 782–865). Master Xuedou Chongxian (Setchō Jūken, 980–1052) also belonged to the Yunmen School which became extinct in the 12th century. He became known as the master who compiled the famous collection of *kōan* named *Biyanlu* (Jap. *Hekiganroku*) and composed the highly poetic verses of praise which elaborate on the hidden punch lines of the respective *kōan*.

5. The Fayan School (Jap. Hōgen School), founded by Fayan Wenyi (Hōgen Bun'eki, 885–958), a lineage which also leads back to the great master Shitou Xiqian. Formative forefathers of this school were Xuefeng Yicun (Seppō Gison, 822–908) and his disciple Xuansha Shibei (Gensha Shibi) who was the actual founder of this school. However, the fame of his dharma grandson Fayan outshone that of Xuansha, so that this school eventually became known as the Fayan School; it became extinct in the 10th century

THE OUTRAGEOUS METHODS OF THE CLASSICAL CHAN MASTERS

The eminent Chan master Deshan Xuanjian, belonging to the generation of masters following Mazu, became famous for his skilful use of the stick. When treasure hunters came to him with questions or to present their insights, he often did not even let them have their say, but scared them off, shouting, "Thirty blows if you have something to say. Thirty blows if you have nothing to say." Baizhang Huaihai, one of the most influential disciples and dharma heirs of master Mazu, himself not prissy when it came to the use of the stick, even had to suffer a slap in the face from his own disciple Huangbo. And Huangbo, for that matter, did not fare better with his closest disciple, Linji Yixuan. To appreciate the outrageousness of this behaviour, we should be aware that respect for old age, and highest esteem for one's teacher belonged to the basic values in traditional Chinese culture and were deeply engrained in every Chinese from childhood on. And Linji, a most cunning fellow, not only perfected the beating with a stick or flywhisk as a means of instructing his disciples, but also became notorious for his use of the cry 'Ho!'

(in Japan in later times 'Katsu!'). Linji himself distinguished four kinds of 'Ho!':

> Sometimes it is like the diamond sword of a vajra king. Sometimes it is like a golden-haired lion sneaking up in a crouch. Sometimes it is like a lure stick with a tuft of grass dangling on the end. Sometimes it is no 'Ho!' at all.

Now what have beatings, kicks, shouts and similarly 'shocking' methods to do with the sublime doctrines of Buddhism, and the Treasury of the Eye of the True Dharma which was preserved by the patriarchs? Let us recall that prince Siddhārtha from the house of Shākya became a Buddha, an 'Awakened One', exactly by this *awakening*. The 'Four Noble Truths', the 'Noble Eightfold Path', the doctrine of dependent origination, as well as of the nonself of all beings and things are, in the end, an expression of this one central experience of awakening or enlightenment. Without *bodhi*, that is awakening, there is no Buddha and no *buddhadharma*, no doctrine of the Awakened One and no path of awakening. No other tradition in the transmission of the *buddhadharma* has taken this obvious fact as seriously, and has implemented it as radically in its methods of instructions and its approach to everyday life, as the Zen tradition.

As Huineng, the Sixth Patriarch, said in his 'Platform Sūtra' in one concise sentence: 'Buddhism is the teaching of nonduality.' And the Zen of the Patriarchs is not about some kind of method, some kind of philosophy, some kind of religion or 'spirituality', some kind of '-ism', but first and foremost about realization of the awakening to this nonduality, the fundamental experience of the Buddha. And thus whatever leads to the realization of this nonduality is 'Buddhism' in its most essential form, no matter in what outwardly, 'non-Buddhist' forms it may manifest. What did Huineng report about the transmission of the *buddhadharma* from the Fifth Patriarch to himself? 'It was just a matter of seeing one's own nature. Meditation and liberation [and other 'Buddhist' questions] were not discussed.'

This is why Deshan did not allow his disciples to indulge themselves in discussions of 'Buddhist questions' right from the beginning. And this is why the methods of instruction of Mazu, Baizhang, Huangbo, Linji and all other masters of Chan and Zen were geared first and foremost to sparking off this 'seeing into one's own nature'. And to come back to the rude methods of these masters: At the end of the

Nonduality (Skrt. *advaita*, Chin. *bu er*, Jap. *fu ni*, literally 'not-two') denotes the state of consciousness that all great spiritual traditions of the world aspire to. It is a state in which dualistic thinking and dualistic perception are transcended (not altogether *eliminated*, but transcended and integrated into a higher state of consciousness). Dualistic consciousness is characterized by the splitting of the ultimate (nondual) reality into two opposed and contradictory categories, the most fundamental split being that into 'subject' and 'object', 'I' and 'Other'. If we project this split onto nondual reality, it endlessly produces other dichotomies like inside and outside, pleasant and unpleasant, being and non-being, life and death, enlightenment and delusion, good and evil.

The subject-object-split is seen as the root of all human suffering, the predicament every human being finds herself in. The Bible calls this event the 'fall of men' which happens precisely by eating from the tree of 'knowledge of good and evil'. This 'knowledge not being wisdom' leads to the expulsion from paradise, the original blissful state of man; our 'original face'. Huineng, the sixth Chinese patriarch of Zen, characterizes the essence of Zen with this statement, 'Buddhism is the teaching of nonduality.' And in his, 'Verses on the Mind of Faith' (*Xinxinming*), one single praise of nonduality, Sengcan, the third Chinese patriarch, sings:

Do not remain in the relative [dualistic] view of things;
Religiously avoid following it.
If there is the slightest trace of 'this' and 'that',
The mind is lost in a maze of complexity.
Duality arises from unity;
But do not be attached to this unity.[15]

quoted stories and countless other anecdotes about similar clashes of a treasure hunter with a master of Zen, we often hear, 'The monk had an insight', or, 'This instant XY experienced awakening'.

TRIGGERS FOR THE EXPERIENCE OF AWAKENING

Even if the consciousness of a human being is ripe for a breakthrough to enlightened comprehension, very often some kind of trigger is necessary for this breakthrough to occur. This can be a very subtle stimulus as, in the case of Shākyamuni Buddha, the blinking of the morning star in the eastern sky, or the scent of plum blossoms wafting in the spring breeze, the sound of a pebble hitting the stem of a bamboo, the clanging sound of a garbage can being shut, or the fluttering of the bright yellow scarf of a fish vendor in a gust of wind. The moment of breakthrough may come as softly and gently as the bursting of the skin of an overripe peach, or with a sudden explosion as with the ripe seed vessel of a jewelweed which projects its seeds all around at the light touch of a cheering child.

If, however, in a person who has reached a certain inner ripeness and disposition towards a breakthrough, the patterns of dualistic thinking, feeling and perceiving are still strongly consolidated due to force of habit, they can function like a dam that resists the breaking through of the floods of enlightened awareness. In such a case a sudden shock like an unexpected blow or kick or shout can cause the barrier to collapse – or can at least rip a gap in the dam.

Most of us have had the experience that a sudden shock, for example when we have an accident or when we hear about the death of a beloved person, can wipe away all of our everyday thoughts, feelings and aspirations, and for a while our mind is blank, a *tabula rasa* or, as is often expressed in Zen, like a piece of 'white paper' (Jap. *hakushi*). Following Mazu, the Chan masters increasingly made use of this experience to break down the barrier of our 'common consciousness' (*bonpu no jōshiki*) or at least to make it permeable for a moment.

But why then does not everybody experience 'enlightenment' when subjected to a sudden shock? Indeed it happens sometimes, in very rare cases, spontaneously and without any preparation to somebody who never had any 'spiritual' aspirations or any formal meditative training. If, however, a shock, a shout, a kick or a good beating alone were sufficient to trigger a breakthrough, enlightenment should be nothing unusual on the streets of our cities. But no, things do not work this way. What most Zen stories about 'stick and shout' leading to a sudden breakthrough do not mention – because it is a matter of course within the Zen context – is the fact that these breakthroughs

Satori, Japanese term (derived from the verb '*satoru*' – to realize) for the experience of awakening or enlightenment, a 'breakthrough' to awakened comprehension.

A synonym for satori is '*kenshō*' (Chin. *jianxing*, literally 'view of self-nature'). Such a breakthrough experience may occur in varying degrees of depth and intensity. Usually Zen masters hold that repeated *kenshō* are necessary before it can come to a 'great satori reaching to the bottom' (Jap. *daigo tettei*).

usually happen after years, if not decades of intensive inner search, and regular meditative training.

If Siddhārtha had stayed in the palace of his father, and if he had covered up his nagging doubts by indulging in luxury, sex and power, or had he just led the life of a respectable family man and become a square instead of a searcher, there would have been little chance that one morning the blinking of Venus in the sky would have triggered his supreme enlightenment. If no mighty flood of the will for truth has gathered behind the barrier of the individual's 'common consciousness', if there is not this dark and nameless longing surging against the dam, if there is no profound urge to arrive at what is 'always already' present, then a jolting of the barrier does not bring about a breaking through the restricting walls of dualistic thinking and perception. Some water may percolate through the dam, or the dam may be deformed under the pressure of overwhelming impressions into more or less pathological mental confines. It may even break down temporarily, leading to the impression that the conventions of society have lost their sway over us, but usually it will be quickly rebuilt, generally with additional pillars and fortifications in order to guarantee more 'security'.

If, however, after years of inner search and meditative training the driving will for truth has become as powerful as, for example in the case of Huike, the second Chinese patriarch, who did not hesitate to cut off his arm so as to convince Bodhidharma to accept him as a disciple, then a single word, one phrase, a gesture or, for that matter, a shout or blow with a stick, may cause the barrier to be blown away, thus opening the view into a new, non-dual dimension of comprehension.

THE DANGER OF THE ABUSE OF UNCONVENTIONAL MEANS

If they are applied at the right moment and in the right state of mind, that of the nondual consciousness of an authentic Zen master, stick and shout can trigger an awakening. The 'if' must be stressed here, since these methods can also be abused. In modern Japan, for example, alongside authentic forms of Zen there exists a kind of 'military Zen' (a degenerated form of discipline which does not really deserve the name 'Zen' and has not really anything to do with the Zen of the Patriarchs), in which the 'awakening stick' (*kyōsaku* or *keisaku*) is used as a device in a kind of barrack yard drill rather than as a skilful means to foster awakening. Just as some big corporations in the West oblige their young management staff to take part in 'survival training' in the wilderness, to toughen them for the merciless war of competition in the market, some social institutions in Japan temporarily dispatch their recruits for hardening to so-called Zen monasteries, where they are thoroughly grilled by stick-wielding monks and grim 'masters' in accordance with the assurance that, 'if it hurts it's doing you good'.

Another form of the abuse of stick and shout, which may be equally detrimental if it is not seen through but is taken seriously, is mere imitation, that in the West, as well as in the East, has led to forms of 'theatre Zen', which may be much admired by naïve believers and New Age adepts, but are as spiritless as a bad copy of a great work of art. A blow with the stick or the flywhisk, or a sudden shout may be the enlightened action of a master. It may, however, also be a puny and theatrical attempt to imitate such action. Then the strike or the 'Ho!' may belong to the fourth of the categories of shouts that Linji mentions, it is 'no "Ho!" at all'.[16] In the *Chuandenglu* we find the following anecdote illustrating this point:

> Once master Muzhou asked a monk about his where and whence. The monk shouted, "Ho!"
>
> Muzhou said, "So you are offering a 'Ho!' to me now."
>
> The monk again shouted: "Ho!"
>
> "Well, well," said Muzhou. "A third 'Ho!' and a fourth 'Ho!', and then what?"
>
> The monk did not know what to answer. Thereupon Muzhou hit him with his stick and said: "Get you gone, you pathetic imitator!"

One thing should be clear by now: with an *authentic* Zen master even such outwardly 'brutal' means of training as kicks and beatings arise from his profound lovingness and not from resentment due to some 'mistake' by, or an inappropriate performance of the disciple. They are by no means some kind of punishment, but rather what Castaneda's Don Juan calls 'ruthless compassion'. To understand this point may be difficult, especially for some Western Zen students who tend towards the attitude, Zen training yes, but only on my own conditions! Needless to say that these conditions are those of the ego, which is precisely the 'imaginary sprout' (as Ramana Maharshi used to call it) that is meant to wither, and eventually to die on the meditation cushion. For the pampered and hypertrophied ego of the contemporary occidental, there is hardly anything more humiliating than to have to submit to a 'beating'. This may be even worse than temporarily accepting the authority of an authentic master and 'obeying' him, an outright scandalous concept for many an upright democrat, especially if one does not understand (and nobody is inclined to explain) why, in Zen training, certain procedures are handled in this way and not in that.

Needless to say to comply with a 'pathetic imitator's'

demand for blind obedience would certainly not be in the best interest of the student. On the other hand, the willingness to suspend one's own opinions, beliefs and predilections under the guidance of an authentic Zen master (who will never demand blind obedience) can be an absolutely necessary prerequisite for the way of Zen. To follow without question the instructions of an authentic master may be as vitally important as it would be for an amateur mountaineer to follow the directions of an experienced mountain guide in critical situations.

But allowing yourself to be hit with a stick? Well, one has to be quite egoless indeed, to take a slap in the face and gleefully laugh about it like the masters Baizhang, Huangbo and other great Zen masters. They cheered with delight at this proof of their disciples' inner freedom, who *finally* had abandoned 'religiously following a dualistic view of things'; who, at long last had transcended hesitation, and all dualistic concepts about 'authority', and who had let go of the difference in importance between master and disciple.

And maybe this challenge to realize the total inner freedom and the cheerful delight of complete egolessness is also contained in the deeper wisdom behind the demand of Jesus Christ to 'turn the other cheek' when slapped.

Out in the fields, Baizhang once asked his disciple Huangbo: "Where have you been?"

Huangbo replied, "I have been gathering mushrooms at the foot of Mount Daxiong [this name means 'Great Calamity']."

Thereupon Baizhang asked, "Have you encountered a tiger?"

Huangbo at once roared like a tiger.

Baizhang picked up an axe from the floor and raised it, as if he wanted to kill the tiger. Thereupon Huangbo slapped him in the face.

Baizhang roared with laughter and returned to the monastery. There he said to the monks: "At the foot of Mount Daxiong there lives a tiger. You monks should beware of him! I have been bitten by him today."

[Tradition has it that Baizhang confirmed Huangbo as his dharma heir with these words.]

From the *Jingde chuandenglu*

7

YOU DON'T TALK WITH A FULL MOUTH

or

From the Zen of the Giants to the Training on the Path of Enlightenment

Yaoshan had not entered the hall to give discourses for quite some time.

The head monk asked him, "The monks have been waiting for a long time now to receive instructions from the master."

Yaoshan said, "Ring the bell."

The monks gathered in the hall.

Thereupon Yaoshan descended from the dharma seat and returned to his room.

The head monk followed him and said, "Master, have you not consented to talk to the monks? Why then didn't you say anything?"

Yaoshan said, "For sūtras *there are* sūtra-*teachers, for* shāstras *there are* shāstra-*teachers. What complaints do you have about me?"*

From the *Jingde Chuandenglu*

Up until the generation of Mazu the staging of the rural farce of the Old Shākya had been a rather exclusive event. Among those who, during the early days of Chan, felt attracted to this kind of play there were obviously only very few who really saw through the plot, and thus could be entrusted with the responsibility to transmit the Treasury of the Eye of the True Dharma. Let us recall that Hongren, the Fifth Patriarch, was already said to have about 1,000 students. It is reasonable to presume that among them there were quite a number of avid treasure hunters like Shenxiu, or like Huiming who eventually was guided to a breakthrough by the Sixth Patriarch on Mount Dayu Ling. But among those 1,000 students there was not a single one who met Hongren's expectations for a dharma heir – until the illiterate barbarian from the south, who was not even an official 'disciple' of the Fifth Patriarch but only a layman working in the kitchen, carried off the treasure.

Let us also recall that after his first encounter with the Fifth Patriarch, Huineng unflinchingly went on chopping wood and pounding rice for a full eight months without receiving any further instructions from Hongren. We may assume that Huineng, at least, could attend some public discourses by the Fifth Patriarch, and the 'Platform Sūtra' also suggests that he did receive some personal advice from Hongren before the Fifth Patriarch handed over the robe and the bowl to him. But nothing in the 'Platform Sūtra' and other early Chan writings indicates that in those times there already existed a systematic 'Zen training' as was developed later on.

THE ZEN OF THE INDIVIDUALISTS

It would not be appropriate to call the early monasteries of Dhyāna Buddhism, like the one that Hongren taught in, 'Chan monasteries'. They were relatively loose congregations of treasure hunters striving for self-realization in the spirit that is described in the *Avatamsaka-sūtra*:

> Sudhana asked, "How does one come to this emancipation face to face?' How does one get this realization?"
>
> Suchandra answered, "A man comes to this emancipation face to face when his mind is awakened to *prajñāpāramitā* and stands in a most intimate relationship to it; for then he attains self-realization in all that he perceives and understands."
>
> Sudhana, "Does one attain self-realization

by listening to the talks and discourses on *prajñāpāramitā*?"

Suchandra, "That is not so. Why? Because *prajñāpāramitā* sees intimately into the truth and reality of all things."

Sudhana, "Is it not that thinking comes from hearing and that by thinking and reasoning one comes to perceive what suchness is? And is this not self-realization?"

Suchandra, "That is not so. Self-realization never comes from mere listening and thinking. O son of a good family, I will illustrate the matter by analogy. Listen! In a great desert there are no springs or wells; in the springtime or in the summer when it is warm, a traveller comes from the west going eastward. He meets a man coming from the east and asks him: 'I am terribly thirsty; pray tell me where I can find a spring and a cool refreshing shade where I might drink, bathe, rest, and get thoroughly revived?'

"The man from the east gives the traveller, as desired, all the information in detail, saying: "When you go further east the road divides itself into two, right and left. You take the right one, and going steadily further on you will surely come to a fine spring and a refreshing shade'. Now, son of a good family, do you think that the thirsty traveller from the west, listening to the talk about a spring and the shady trees, and thinking of going to that place as quickly as possible can be relieved of his thirst and heat and get refreshed?"

Sudhana, "No, he cannot; because he is relieved of thirst and heat and gets refreshed only when, as directed by the other, he actually reaches the fountain and drinks of it and bathes in it."

Suchandra, "Son of a good family, even so with the Bodhisattva. By merely listening to it, thinking of it, and intellectually understanding it, you will never come to the realization of any truth. Son of a good family, the desert means birth and death; the man from the west means all sentient beings; the heat means all forms of confusion; thirst is greed and lust; the man from the east who knows the way is the Buddha or the Bodhisattva who, abiding in all-knowledge has penetrated into the true nature of all things

> and the reality of sameness; to quench the thirst and to be relieved of the heat by drinking of the refreshing fountain means the realization of the truth by oneself."[17]

Now this 'realization of the truth by oneself' through the awakening, which is the hallmark of a 'Buddha', is exactly what all followers of Shākyamuni Buddha aspire to, if they want to be 'real' Buddhists. And this awakening is, in the text quoted above, what is meant by 'self-realization', not the assertion, repudiated by the Buddha, of the Hindu concept of the existence of a 'self' (*ātman*). This must be emphasized, since some avid champions of a 'pure original Buddhism' like to construct a contradiction between Zen and 'real Buddhism' on the grounds of the occasional use of the term 'self-realization' in Zen literature. In doing so, they are attached to provisional terms and concepts, unlike the masters of Zen who have demonstrated again and again that *all* cherished concepts of the 'truth' are ultimately wrong, whether they may be positive or negative formulations.

Likewise it would be wrong to say that by the realization of the Treasury of the Eye of the True Dharma something is 'made real' that would have been 'unreal' before. Nevertheless, it only becomes 'real' for anyone when we awaken to it *ourselves*. The Hassidim, and other spiritual traditions, compare the truth of our own true nature, or original face, (as long as it is unrealized) to a treasure that lies buried in the cave of our own house without us knowing it is there and belonging to us. As long as we do not discover this treasure and manage to unearth it, we may live in this house in bitter poverty, *even though* the treasure is ours all of the time. Only when we dig it up does the treasure become 'real' to us and we can make use of it.

The 'spade' for digging up the treasure is what the Buddha did under the Bodhi Tree, the sitting in meditative absorption, or *dhyāna*. This is the one point all followers of Dhyāna Buddhism in China agreed upon, even if they did not belong to the lineage of transmission that traces itself back via Huineng and Bodhidharma, to Mahākāshyapa and Shākyamuni Buddha. So in the early monasteries of Dhyāna Buddhism one found treasure hunters from diverse traditions, and some of the early Chan masters were, so to say, 'masters-in-residence' in monasteries of other Buddhist schools. These were already established in China when Chan started to develop, and the early Chan masters sometimes 'taught' there alongside masters from

Zazen (Chin. *zuochan*), literally 'to sit' (*za*) in 'meditative absorption' (*zen*) is *the* central practice of Zen and is regarded as the shortest way to awakening.

Zazen should be distinguished from 'meditation' as it is customarily understood. Meditation in general is meditation *on* some object of meditation. This object may be an abstract idea like 'impermanence' or 'compassion'; it may be a sound or an image (mantras, mandalas, visualizations etc.) or some tangible thing that serves as the focus of attention.

Zazen, however, is meant to free the mind from the slavery of *any* thought form, vision, thing or concept, however lofty or 'holy' it may be. Thus even media of practice like the *kōan* are not objects of meditation in the conventional sense. The practitioner rather aspires to become *one* with the *kōan*, to reach a state of absorption (*samādhi*) in which there no longer exists a subject-object split, and thus there is no 'object'. In its purest form *zazen* is a state of thought-free, wide-awake awareness which is not directed towards any object and which is not attached to any 'content'. (*See* Huineng's 'non-abiding', p. 100) other schools. Those masters, from time to time, gave some hints as to where the 'spring and refreshing shade' were to be found. But each wanderer had to hike there by himself and had to drink from the well and bathe in the water himself.

Thus the monks in these early monasteries largely trained themselves on their own, alone in their cell or in a hermitage or a cave in the vicinity of a monastery, much like the famous 'dharma bum' Hanshan, the man from Cold Mountain, who sang about his lonely life in poems that he wrote on rocks, trees and the walls of houses while he was 'free and easy wandering'. It was nothing unusual that, for several months, these monks had no contact with the abbot or Chan master of the monastery to which they were connected. Often they wandered about the country as mendicants without affiliation to any master or monastery.

Linji, for example, the outstanding disciple of Huangbo, who later on became the founder of the Linji School of Zen, had already spent three years in Huangbo's monastery without calling on the master, when his dharma brother Muzhou recognized his talent and urged him to go and meet the master. At this point in Linji's search, the floods of the will to truth surging against the dam of his common consciousness, had

Dokusan, Jap. literally 'alone' (*doku*) 'go to a high one' (Sino-Jap. *san*), a private interview of a Zen disciple with his master in the privacy of the master's room, Dokusan is one of the most important elements of systematic Zen training. It gives the disciple the opportunity to talk about all problems he may have with his practice and to demonstrate to the master in confidence where he stands in his comprehension of the truth, for example by presenting his response to a *kōan* to him. According to the tradition of Zen this individual tuition has its roots in the 'secret instructions' of Shākyamuni Buddha.

already gathered so much force, that a few nudges from Huangbo and his stick, and a little help from his friend Muzhou, were sufficient to trigger a breakthrough in him.

But treasure hunters with a will to truth like Huineng or Linji – not to mention Huike, who chopped off one of his arms to convince Bodhidharma of the seriousness of his aspiration – were scarce. In all seriousness which of us would cut off an arm in the hope of gaining something as literally unimaginable as 'enlightenment'? A most promising word, indeed, but who knows whether it is worthwhile to, 'drop off body and mind' (as Tiantong Ruji, the Chinese master of Dōgen Zenji put it) to gain something as immeasurable as this awakening. And all the more so, since no authentic master can guarantee that our efforts really will lead within this life (and not maybe in a few *kalpas*) to the goal for which we are striving. Maybe then, it might be better to stay with what we know already and not to walk on the wild side? Not only in Hongren's monastery were there quite a few that did not dare to jump into the unknown.

But does this mean that, for us less daring people, the access to the central experience of Zen, to satori, or awakening, is forever barred? Not necessarily. Fortunately, the Chinese Zen masters have developed 'skilful means' to lure people less gifted than the Chan masters of the Golden Age, out of the comfort zone of their common consciousness.

THE TRAINING TRICKS OF THE CHAN MASTERS

One prerequisite for the development of Chan-specific training methods was the emergence of increasingly Chan-specific monasteries. Mazu's disciple, Baizhang Huaihai, played an important part in this development by setting up exact rules for the life and the daily schedule of a Zen monastery, rules that were specifically adapted to the requirements of training on the path of Zen. By and large these rules determine the daily life in Zen monasteries even until today.

Baizhang expressed one of those rules, a rule that had already been set up by Daoxin, the fourth Chinese patriarch, for the daily life of his 500 followers, and which would soon prove to be very beneficial for the survival of Chan. His famous dictum states, 'A day without work, a day without a meal'. According to the rules which had been adopted from the Indian Sangha, living under climatically quite different conditions, Buddhist monks in China up to that point had been forbidden to take care of material concerns. The monasteries lived on the alms of the laity, offerings from rich benefactors, and not least, on donations from sovereigns. Some like the emperor Wu of Liang, hoped to gain good karma, or, as was not unusual in ancient China, were themselves disciples of outstanding Buddhist masters.

Now the Chan monasteries increasingly became self-sufficient communities, which provided for their livelihood by the work of their own hands. A famous episode from the monastery of Baizhang shows how seriously the master himself took the rules that he had set up. When the master was well advanced in years, his monks were afraid that he may have become too frail for the hard work in the fields, and therefore hid his farming tools. From that moment on Baizhang refused to eat until his tools reappeared and he could partake in the daily work again. This attitude, and the resulting independence of the Chan communities, (which usually lived in remote areas far away from the centres of power, often on a mountain whose name later on would become the name of the founder of that monastery) were a decisive reason for the survival of the Chan communities during the great persecution of Buddhists under the reign of emperor Wuzong (841–46). The Chan monasteries weathered this persecution better than most other Buddhist monasteries, and this fact contributed to Chan becoming the predominant Buddhist tradition in China in consecutive centuries. But, beneficial as the regulated daily schedule in a Chan monastery may have been for the spiritual training of the monks, the decisive steps on the path had to be taken by each practitioner on his own. To facilitate and to assist this process, the ancient Chan masters came up with a number of ingenious training tricks. In the beginning, these gestures were certainly not consciously adopted *methods*, but spontaneous responses. The masters reacted without any deliberation to the state of mind of the disciple.

Mazu's shouts, blows and kicks were but the most spectacular of these gestures. Other means to bring the interfering discursive thought process, which maintains our common consciousness, to a halt, at least for a few moments, (and often *the* decisive moments) and thus to facilitate the breakthrough of something quite different, were surprising wordless gestures, made for example with the traditional flywhisk of the Buddhist monk. Or the master would suddenly call the disciple by name when he was about to turn around and leave, another trick first used by Mazu. Most people react instantly and without thinking when their name is called. We all have had this experience of spontaneous reaction when on the street or in an anonymous crowd someone calls a friend, or a child, by their first name, and this name happens to be our name. When the disciple turned around, the master would drive the wedge of a thunderous "What is this!' into the gap that had momentarily opened up in the thought process of the disciple.

To jolt a disciple out of the sleep of his common consciousness the early Chan masters would also hurl an unexpected and 'paradoxical' answer to an urgent question about the essence of Zen experience at the monk:

> A monk asked Shitou, "Why did the First Patriarch come from the West?"
>
> Shitou said, "Ask the temple pillar over there."
>
> The monk said, "I do not understand."
>
> Shitou said, "Neither do I."

> The layman Pang asked master Mazu, "What kind of a man is it, who has no counterpart among men?"
>
> Mazu said, "I will tell you, once you have swallowed the waters of the West River with one gulp."
>
> Hearing this, Pang Yun suddenly comprehended the essence of Chan.

A monk asked master Zhaozhou, "Who is the Buddha?"

Zhaozhou said, "The one there in the shrine."

The monk asked, "But is that sitting there in the shrine not just a figure made of clay?"

"Yes, that is right."

"But who then is Buddha?"

Zhaozhou replied, "The one there in the shrine."

A monk asked, "If all things return to the One, where does the One return to?"

Master Zhaozhou replied: "When I was staying at Jinzhou, I made myself a robe that weighed seven pounds."

These fishhooks of the Chan masters were paradoxical for one simple reason, they flowed directly from the enlightened, non-dual consciousness of these masters, and thus could not be understood (and can never be understood) by discursive thinking, which is always restricted to the domain of duality. They were invitations or challenges to swallow this bait from another dimension of consciousness and, thrashing on the line of the master, be projected into the vast emptiness of awakened comprehension.

Accordingly only those replies that were on a par with the challenge were accepted as valid replies:

> Master Mazu once stepped in front of the gathering of monks and dwelled in silence for a long while.
>
> Baizhang rolled up the mat in front of his seat.
>
> Thereupon the master left the lecture hall.

— ☯ —

> When Caoshan was taking leave of Dongshan, Dongshan asked him, "Where do you want to go?"
>
> "I am going to where there is no change."
>
> "How do you want to go to where there is no change?"
>
> "My going is no change."

— ☯ —

> Master Caoshan once asked a monk, what he was doing. The monk answered, "I am sweeping the floor."
>
> The master asked, "Are you sweeping in

front of the Buddha or behind the Buddha?"

The monk answered, "I am sweeping both places at once."

Thereupon Caoshan said, "Go and fetch my slippers."

Once, when master Weishan was lying on his bed, Yangshan entered his room to talk to him, but the master turned his face to the wall. Yangshan said, "How can you do that?"

The master got up and said, "A few moments ago I had a dream. Won't you try to interpret it for me?"

Thereupon Yangshan brought a bowl of water for the master to wash his face.

A little later Xiangyan also entered to talk to the master.

The master said, "I just had a dream. Yangshan has already interpreted it for me. Now it is your turn."

Xiangyan brought him a cup of tea. The master said, "The insight of you two even surpasses that of Shāriputra [the brightest among the close disciples of the Buddha]."

The reply to the challenge of a Zen master must occur as direct and spontaneously as the challenge itself. Any deliberated reply is at once seen through and rejected by an authentic master:

> Yunyan came to see master Guizong. Guizong made the gesture of aiming at him with a drawn bow.
>
> After a long pause Yunyan made the gesture of drawing a sword.
>
> Guizong said, "Too late!"

— ☯ —

> Master Muzhou heard about an old Chan master who gave himself the air of being totally unapproachable.
>
> When the old Chan master saw Muzhou entering his room, he immediately shouted his, "Ho!"
>
> Muzhou slapped him with his hand and said, "Nothing but imitation!"

— ☯ —

> The master Dongshan Liangjie once said to the abbot of Tai, "There is something which

props up the sky above and maintains the earth below. It is constantly in action and as black as tar. Is there anything wrong about it?"

The abbot answered, "The fault is in its activity."

The master shouted: "Get lost!"

A monk came to see master Muzhou. Muzhou asked him, "Aren't you one of those monks who keep wandering all around the country?"

The monk said, "Yes."

The master asked, "Have you already prostrated in front of the Buddha statue?"

The monk replied, "Why should I bow down in front of a lump of clay?"

The master shouted, "Get lost at once and treat yourself to a good thrashing!"

Yes, in those days too, there already existed 'theatre Zen', not in the sense of the rural farce of the Old Shākya, or the spontaneous slapstick stagings of the Chan masters, but as mere imitations of 'dramatic' gestures. So somebody who has heard of masters urging their disciples to 'kill the Buddha, when you meet him', of Zen monks who did not hesitate to take a wooden Buddha statue for firewood when they were cold, or of famous masters who answered to the question, 'What is Buddha?' with 'A piece of dried shit' may assume that 'Why should I bow down in front of a lump of clay?' is a downright 'zenny' answer.

NO ICONOCLASM, NO SHOW EFFECT

Zen, however, is no mere iconoclasm. The Chan masters were not only aiming at smashing all 'graven images' in the mind of their disciples that might get in the way of a direct apprehension of reality. They were not only up to eradicating all discursive concepts of something 'holy' or 'exalted' which exists as the 'really real', apart from, beyond or *above* everyday reality. It was of even greater importance to them to bring their disciples to the point of experiencing that the holy, the essential '*buddha-nature*', is completely manifested at any moment in any thing, and that, as Hongren said, 'every thing in its true nature incorporates the *whole* truth'.

The 'Buddha', about which the monk is asking master Zhaozhou, (*see* Page 147) is just a concept, an image in the mind of the monk. Thus, Zhaozhou's first response, 'The one there in the shrine', is immediately mirroring the limited understanding of the monk. But when the monk insists, Zhaozhou, in his grandfatherly kindliness, stresses the other aspect of his genial response with his second answer, 'The one there in the shrine'. The text does not tell us whether the monk was able to grasp this Living Buddha at this moment.

For that matter, the monk who comes to call on master Muzhou in the anecdote quoted on page 150, obviously has not comprehended, and accordingly does not understand that the master is not really asking him whether the wandering monk, upon his arrival in the monastery, has already complied with the formal ritual of prostrating in front of the Buddha image. Thus, the monk is not able to answer from the point of view of genuine Zen experience, but has to resort to 'hearsay', an answer that he *thinks* is 'zenny' and with which he tries to belie his ignorance.

But the monk underestimates Muzhou who cannot be deceived so easily. One who is ignorant, and does not know he is ignorant, is not likely to call on a Zen master. One who is ignorant and knows he is ignorant, may knock at the door of a Zen master as a sincere treasure hunter, and the master may have the ruthless compassion to chase him away with blows of his stick, if this is what the seeker needs at this moment. But if someone is simply concerned to make an impression, and pretend that he knows, even though he is ignorant, on such a person Muzhou does not even want to soil his stick. Thus he advises the monk, who is not inclined to bow down to *buddha-nature* (that is his *own* nature) in the form of a lump of clay, to treat himself to a good thrashing. Well, yes, they could be pretty rough on 'pathetic imitators', these old Chan masters.

But apart from counterfeit monks, what could be done to help those treasure hunters who were, in all sincerity, searching for the Treasury of the Eye of the True Dharma, but who were not driven by the overwhelming will to truth of the early Chan masters, which, in the case of those giants of Zen, led to a state of mind that needed only a small nudge to propel them into a breakthrough to awakened comprehension? In most schools of Buddhism, but especially in Dhyāna Buddhism, the basic and indispensable medium of inner maturation was, and is, meditation, which is practised in Zen in its most essential Form. This 'sitting in absorption' (or what Zhuangzi used to call 'sitting and forgetting') is today, known as '*zazen*'. This practice is the fertile ground, the sunshine and the moistening rain that brings the fruit of the mind to maturation.

Depending on the predisposition, however, of the individual practitioner, this process of maturation may proceed so slowly that in view of the scarcity of time that this precious incarnation as a human being provides, a dose of 'fertilizer' to speed up the process may be most helpful.

As the most effective of these accelerators of growth, the Chan masters, who were the heirs of pioneers and innovators like Mazu, Baizhang or Shitou, developed the use of the *gongan* (Jap. *kōan*), that kind of Korfian joke with delayed ignition (see page 62), the punch line of which only dawns on us in the deepest night of our common consciousness.

A thousand lives, ten thousand deaths –
how long shall this keep going on?
Being born and dying, coming and going –
from defilement to darkness deep.
They do not see within their own hearts
the priceless jewel they own –
Still they are like a blind donkey
obediently trotting along.

Hanshan, 'Poems from Cold Mountain'

8

THE BARRIER OF THE PATRIARCHS

or

Kōan Practice and the Leap into the Abyss of Not-Knowing

I have nothing to say –
and I am saying it.

John Cage

'A thousand lives, ten thousand deaths, how long shall this keep going on?' Whoever is haunted by this question, like Hanshan and countless human beings before and after him, and who is longing for a way out of *samsāra*, the 'cycle of birth and death', may become a searcher on the inner path – as did the prince Siddhārtha. As we said in the beginning of this book, the 'spiritual career' of Gautama Buddha, the Awakened One, in many respects is paradigmatic or exemplary for the way of liberation.

Most searchers in the beginning try to reach their 'aim' with the help of philosophies, practices and methods. Quite a few of them soon are so much in love with one of these techniques, that it becomes an end in itself, and thus a serious impediment for the realization of the liberation to which they are aspiring. You can easily spend your whole life in the study of spiritual teachings, philosophies, systems, theologies and buddhologies, and might even become a super-practitioner or a record meditator, without ever coming to the point of standing alone (or all-one) with no crutches, the point at which Zen begins.

For practically all searchers who eventually reach liberation, there is no getting around the experience (which probably was the bitterest pill for Siddhārtha, the seeker, to swallow) that nothing, precisely no-thing at all that we can think or do, can bestow liberation on us. And this often dawns on a seeker only after years or even decades of 'spiritual training', throughout which the seeker has made many sacrifices, and has 'done' everything in his power to reach that goal. And must that not be dire? Must it not pitch the searcher into deepest desperation? Well, it has often done exactly that, and it is not seldom that this dark night of the soul, this state of utter desolation, precedes a breakthrough to awakening.

It just seems to be part and parcel of the personality of us human beings that we're only ready to make the last sacrifice, when in the deepest inner distress. This 'last sacrifice' means letting go of *everything* that we cling to, of all fear *and* all hope, of everything we assume to be able to do or to be, and to jump into the abyss of not-knowing and not-doing. It may also be, however, that we really 'make' no sacrifice at all; that we just reach a point where we are simply too exhausted, too despondent to try any longer to do, or to want, or to be anything, so that we 'drop off body and mind' or rather, that 'body and mind fall away' because we do not have the strength to hold on to them any longer.

THE RUTHLESS COMPASSION OF THE MASTERS

Knowing very well how crucial this state of desperation, of utter despondency can be as a springboard to the experience of a breakthrough, more and more of the heirs of the Chan masters Mazu & Co. out of deep compassion with their disciples, decided to reduce them to total despair. The skilful means for helping them to achieve this was the *gongan* (*kōan*), the original meaning of this Chinese word being a 'judicial precedent'.

For such precedents the Chan masters used sayings and episodes from the biographies of earlier masters; sometimes also paradoxical phrases from a *sūtra*. It is exactly this paradoxical element of a *kōan*, that which is 'beyond thought' (Greek *para dokein*), which is the essential point. The master challenges the disciple to demonstrate his or her understanding of this precedent, but the essential points of a *kōan* just *cannot* be understood. If what is presented is mere 'understanding', an authentic master rejects it as not being to the point. This way the master puts the disciple into an impossible situation, he demands the disciple to deliver something, which he, with every means and ability known to him so far, cannot possibly deliver. The master claims and knows, from his own experience, that there *is* a 'solution', and he insists ruthlessly, without any pity, that the disciple present his solution in word and/or deed. He tells him a joke and withholds the punch line, because to give it away would mean to deprive the disciple of this priceless moment, when the punch line dawns on him for himself, in an inner explosion of sudden comprehension that propels him, with a liberating laughter, into a new perception of reality, the non-dual perception, by which alone, as master Dōgen once said, the world becomes real.

We already noted that it is the dam of the common consciousness, which blocks the entry into the awakened dimension of comprehension. This barrier is a nearly impenetrable tangle of ideas, views, notions, concepts, habits and dualistic thoughts and feelings, a *huge* dam of boulders, scree and rubble in which the trickle of our normal meditative efforts usually just seeps away, even if we keep it running by continued *zazen*. We may keep it up as long as we want; it is not strong enough to burst the barrier that blocks our vision. But even the smallest trickle may swell to a mighty flood with the help of 'skilful means' – by building a dam that proves to be an impenetrable barrier for our will to truth. The *kōan* is such a dam, and indeed, in Zen, is sometimes called 'the barrier of the patriarchs'.

We have already encountered some of these barriers in the preceding chapter. Basically each saying or action that directly flows out of non-dual consciousness, that is awakened awareness, is apt to serve as a *kōan*. The essential core, the punch line of such a precedent can only be 'comprehended' if one jumps out of the dualistic common consciousness onto the plane of non-dual experience. The term 'comprehension' is used here instead of 'understanding', since to comprehend, in its root meaning, denotes a kind of 'grasping', which is much closer to the almost physical experience of really touching, and taking hold of the core of a *kōan*, than mere intellectual understanding.

Nevertheless, there are precedents that are especially

appropriate to serving as a 'barrier of the patriarchs', and that have been used for centuries as a means of training treasure hunters on the path of Zen. Beginning with the 12th century these *kōan* have been compiled into collections that were meant to serve as 'manuals' of Zen training. In these collections they often were accompanied by hints, pointers, marginal notes, short discourses (which are not 'commentaries' in the academic sense of the word), and sometimes a poem of praise, which highlights the essential points of the *kōan* and often itself constitutes or contains a further *kōan*. The *Wumenguan* (Jap. *Mumonkan*, 'The Gateless Barrier'), the *Biyanlu* (Jap. *Hekiganroku*, 'The Blue Cliff Record') and the *Congronglu* (Jap. *Shōyōroku*, 'The Record [from the Hermitage] of Serenity') are only the best known of these collections. There exist several others, including those from the tradition of the Caodong School (Jap. Sōtō School) of Zen, that allegedly does not work with *kōan*. Here are some typical examples of such 'barriers' from the collection that for a good reason is called 'The Gateless Barrier' (*Wumenguan*):[18]

> The priest Xiangyan said, "It is as though you were up in a tree, hanging from a branch with your teeth. Your hands and feet can't touch

any branch. Someone appears beneath the tree and asks, 'What is the meaning of Bodhidharma's coming from the West?'. If you do not answer, you evade your responsibility. If you do answer, you lose your life. What do you do?"

— ☯ —

A monk said to Caoshan, "I am Qingshui, lonely and poor. Please give me alms."

Caoshan said, "Venerable Shui!"

Qingshui said, "Yes, sir!"

Caoshan said, "You have already drunk three cups of the finest wine in China, and still you say that you have not moistened your lips."

— ☯ —

Zhaozhou went to a hermit's cottage and asked, "Anybody in? Anybody in?" The hermit lifted up his fist.

Zhaozhou said, "The water is too shallow for a ship to anchor." And he left.

Again he went to a hermit's cottage and asked, "Anybody in? Anybody in?"

This hermit too lifted up his fist.

Zhaozhou said, "Freely you give, freely you take away, freely you kill, freely you give life." And he made a full bow.

A monk asked Dongshan, "What is Buddha?"

Dongshan said, "Three pounds of flax."

The priest Songyuan asked, "Why can't the person of great strength lift his legs and get up?"

Again he said, "He speaks without using his tongue."

The priest Shishuang said, "How can you proceed beyond the tip of a hundred-foot pole?"

Zen practice with a *kōan* usually begins quite harmless. The disciple is asked to attend to the inspection of the *kōan* and to answer the question(s) contained therein or to demonstrate the crucial point(s) of the *kōan* in words and deeds. The disciple, who hitherto knows no other way of comprehension than his intellect, at first tries to understand the *kōan* with his discursive thinking and gives all kinds of answers from his head. D T Suzuki writes:

> The method of *kōan* practice … consists in eradicating all traces of discursive intellection by sheer power of will, whereby the Zen students prepare their consciousness to provide the suitable ground for the breakthrough of intuitive knowledge. They try to find their way through a forest of concepts that encroach upon their mind like a thicket of twines.

But each and every response that is born out of the mind, out of discursive thinking, is immediately wiped away by the master, "No, far off the point! WHAT is the essential point of your *kōan*?" To characterize the challenge to the Zen disciple, D T Suzuki first quotes master Dahui Zonggao (1089–1163), who was a passionate champion of *kōan* practice …

> This matter is like a great mass of fire; when you approach it your face is sure to be scorched. It is again like a sword about to be

> drawn; when it is out of the scabbard, someone is sure to lose his life. But if you neither fling away the scabbard nor approach the fire, you are no better than a piece of rock or wood. Coming to this pass, one has to be quite a resolute character, full of spirit.

... and then he concludes:

> There is nothing here suggestive of cool reasoning and quiet metaphysical or epistemological analysis, but of a certain desperate will to break through an insurmountable barrier, of the will impelled by some irrational or unconscious power behind it. Therefore the outcome also defies intellection or conceptualization.[19]

When all 'explanations' produced by the intellect or conceptualizations are exhausted, this 'unconscious power' slowly begins to gather behind the insurmountable dam. The flood retained by the barrier of the patriarch begins to rise; the inner pressure that demands a resolution increases. Now the disciple may begin to guess, to helplessly grope around in a thick fog that seems to have swallowed up his reasoning, or he may hold his tongue in deep perplexity, or because he now believes the answer is silence. But the master obstinately *insists* on an answer.

Slowly but surely the question becomes more and more tantalizing. Again and again the practitioner attacks the *kōan* that rises in front of him like an impenetrable 'iron wall'. Again and again he tries to surmount the barrier, but it is like a 'silver mountain' with steep slopes so smooth that he finds no foothold. Master Dahui describes this phase of his own *kōan* practice like this: 'My position is that of a dog which stands by a fat-boiling pot: he cannot lick it however badly he wants to, nor can he go away from it though he may wish to quit.'[20] And to urge the disciple on once more the Japanese Master Shōichi Kokushi advises him:

> Think yourself to be down an old deep well;
> the only thought you then have will be to get
> out of it, and you will be desperately engaged
> in finding a way of escape; from morning to
> evening this one thought will occupy the
> entire field of your consciousness.

When one has reached this stage of the practice, the resolution of the *kōan* begins to take on an existential urgency; like the escape from the deep well, it becomes a question of life and death. The practitioner feels like he is choking on the question. With increasing strain he pants for the air of comprehension, but the *kōan* is stuck in his throat like a 'red-hot iron ball' that he cannot swallow or vomit out.

All these images are not just flowery metaphors, but are expressions of a very concrete agony that those, who have struggled with a *kōan*, have suffered. And as if they took a sadistic delight in torturing their disciples, the masters drive their disciples deeper and deeper into this bottomless distress, into this desolation beyond all bearing. They know that the deepest resources within their disciples, powers which enable them to break through to awakened comprehension, are only activated in this utter despondency; that the dam of the common consciousness can only crumble and be washed away if the power of the floods pushing against the barrier of the patriarchs has reached an intensity that just cannot be contained any more.

FROM THE DARK NIGHT TO THE BRIGHT LIGHT OF COMPREHENSION

In the course of many centuries of Zen practice the famous 'Kōan Mu' has proven to be one of the most effective means of bringing Zen practitioners to their first *kenshō* experience, which usually has to be followed up by many consecutive breakthroughs, that deepen and widen this first hint of 'enlightenment'. This *kōan* is the first case in the famous *Wumenguan*, the 'Gateless Barrier':

> A monk asked Zhaozhou, "Does a dog have *buddha-nature* or not?"
> Zhaozhou said, "Wu." [Jap. Mu]

'Wu', is a negation, and in normal usage it means 'no', 'is not', 'has not' or 'nothing'. But as the person practising with the *kōan* finds out in the course of his or her efforts, 'Wu', in this case, does not have this literal meaning. In his short discourse on this *kōan*, the Chinese master Wumen Huikai, who compiled the *Wumenguan*, does not only indicate how one is supposed to practise with the 'Kōan Mu' (and other *kōan*), but also summarizes the inner process of the struggle with the *kōan*, right up to its solution:

> For the practice of Zen it is imperative that you pass through the barrier set up by the Ancestral Teachers. For subtle realization it is of the utmost importance that you cut off the mind road. If you do not pass the barrier of the ancestors, if you do not cut off the mind road, then you are a ghost clinging to bushes and grasses.
>
> What is the barrier of the Ancestral Teachers? It is just this one word 'Mu' – the one barrier of our faith. We call it the Gateless Barrier of the Zen tradition. When you pass through this barrier you will not only interview Zhaozhou intimately. You will walk hand in hand with the Ancestral Teachers in the successive generations of our lineage, the hair of your eyebrows entangled with theirs, seeing with the same eyes, hearing with the same ears. Won't that be fulfilling? Is there anyone who would not want to pass this barrier?
>
> So, then, make your whole body a mass of doubt, and with your three hundred and sixty

bones and joints and your eighty-four thousand hair follicles concentrate on this one word 'Mu'. Day and night, keep digging into it. Don't consider it to be nothingness. Don't think of it in terms of 'has' and 'has not'. It is like swallowing a red-hot iron ball. You try to vomit it out, but you can't.

Gradually you purify yourself, eliminating mistaken knowledge and attitudes you have held from the past. Inside and outside become one. You're like a mute person who has a dream; you know it for yourself alone.

Suddenly Mu breaks open. The heavens are astonished, the earth is shaken. It is as though you have snatched the great sword of general Guan. When you meet the Buddha, you kill the Buddha. When you meet Bodhidharma, you kill Bodhidharma. At the very cliff edge of birth-and-death, you find the Great Freedom. In the Six Worlds and the Four Modes of Birth, you enjoy a samādhi of frolic and play.

How, then, should you work with it? Exhaust all your energy on this one word, 'Mu'. If you do not falter, then it's done. A single spark lights your *dharma* candle.[21]

With the lighting of this *dharma* candle by 'one spark', the Zen practitioner is sitting hand in hand with Buddha under the Bodhi Tree and experiences the lighting of his *dharma* candle by the blinking of the Morning Star – to see with the same eyes and hear with the same ears. Once again a cycle is completed and a human being has entered the dimensionless point of the transmission of the Treasury of the Eye of the True Dharma. And where has he arrived? At the point at which, like the old masters emphasize, the Zen training now really can *begin*.

Green creek – the water from the source
is limpid.
Cold Mountain – the halo of the moon
is white.
Silent illumination, the mind is realized
by itself.
Knowing the void, delusion turns into
tranquillity.

Hanshan, 'Poems from Cold Mountain'

EPILOGUE

or

Zen in the West

There is nothing to it,
unless you do it.

Erich Kästner

With the development of the skilful means of Zen training by the Chinese Chan masters of the Tang and Song dynasties, the Zen tradition had accomplished its full maturation. All further developments within the world of Zen are but 'footnotes' to this Golden Age of Zen. But as the fall from the tree, and the rotting on the earth, is already implicit in the ripe fruit, even in this heyday of Chan the first signs of decay were already evident. And as the sprout of the new plant springs forth from the rotting fruit, after the decline of Chinese Chan there have been new blooms of the *dharma* of the patriarchs in the forms of the Korean 'Son', and the Japanese 'Zen'. The exuberant vitality of Chan, however, which within a few generations produced dozens of outstanding Chan masters, and hundreds of quite remarkable masters, as well as countless upright treasure hunters who were touched by the 'spirit of Zen' – artists, intellectuals, statesmen and other laymen, drawn from all walks of life – has never been reached since in any other culture or age. This is why this exploration of the essential points of Zen closes at this point.

THE DEPARTURE FROM LIFE AND EXPERIENCE

Since, as we said in the beginning, this book is about what Zen can mean *here and now* to people from the West, in this epilogue a few remarks may be admissible concerning this aspect of the decline of the Zen tradition that is already visible in its embryonic state in the West. Zen will only be able to live in the West, if these seeds of decay are heeded right from the beginning, since they fall on very fertile soil here. D T Suzuki writes in view of this aspect:

> This degeneration, this departure from life and experience, is a phenomenon everywhere observable in the history of religion. There is always in the beginning a creative genius, and

a system grows out of his experiences. People of lesser capacity are gathered about him; he endeavours to make them go through the same experiences as his own; he succeeds in some cases, but failures generally exceed successes. Because most of us are not original and creative enough, we are satisfied with following the steps of a leader who appears to us to be so great and distant. The system thus gradually becomes ossified, and unless there follows a period of revival, the original experiences rapidly die away. In the Chinese history of Zen, this period of decline, we can say, came with the invention of the *kōan* exercise, although it is quite true that this invention was something inevitable in the history of Zen consciousness.

What the *kōan* proposes to do is to develop artificially or systematically in the consciousness of the Zen followers what early masters produced in themselves spontaneously. It also aspires to develop this Zen experience in a greater number of minds than the master could otherwise hope for. Thus, the *kōan* tended to the popularization of

> Zen and at the same time became the means of conserving the Zen experience in its genuineness. Aristocratic Zen was now turned into a democratic, systematized and, to a certain extent, mechanized Zen. [22]

'Didn't we say so all along?' is what some champions of Sōtō Zen may exclaim now. It must be remembered that his was the important school of Zen Buddhism in which many adherents viewed *kōan* practice with certain scepticism, if not with outright disdain. The Caodong School (Jap. Sōtō), and the Linji School (Jap. Rinzai), are the only two of the Five Houses of Zen in China (*see* p112) that have survived, to a certain extent, until the present day.

THE TWO SIDES OF THE MEDAL OF ZEN

The accentuation of a supposed contradiction, however, between Rinzai Zen as Kōan Zen, and Sōtō Zen as Shikantaza Zen (Jap. *shikantaza* – 'nothing but aptly sitting'), is as little valid and helpful as is the distinction between 'sudden' and 'gradual', already discussed in the chapter on Huineng, the Sixth Patriarch. Let us remember that Huineng, who is regarded as *the* foremost proponent of the 'school of sudden illumination', himself said, 'But he who grasps the original mind himself and sees his essential nature knows that (this) distinction does not exist. This is why "sudden" and "gradual" are only provisional concepts.' If we, however, religiously cling to such provisional concepts, they tend to obscure the fact that these two traditions only emphasize *two different aspects* of genuine Zen training, aspects which play an important role in *both* traditions and which only in their inseparable unity, make up the two sides of the medal of genuine Zen practice.

Both traditions may claim that they are based on the authority of the Buddha. Adherents of Rinzai Zen may say: 'Awakening is *the* central experience of the Buddha, the incidence that qualified him as a Buddha, an Awakened One. Without *bodhi*, awakening or "enlightenment", there is no Buddha, no Buddhism and thus no Zen Buddhism. This is why it is indispensable to spur on the development of the Zen adept until he or she reaches *kenshō*, satori or enlightenment, albeit with "artificial" means like the *kōan*. And let's note that every kind of *systematic* meditation advocated in Buddhism may be regarded as an artificial means. All further development of the Zen adept builds on this central experience, which is the Alpha and Omega of Buddhism.'

In arguing that way, adherents of Rinzai Zen emphasize the aspect of the 'relative Truth', what in Buddhism is called *savriti satya* or 'conventional truth'. This is that aspect of non-dual truth which is valid in the phenomenal world, in the world of space and time, and thus of the 'development' of a human being which we always encounter in the phenomenal world of our ordinary experience, whether this human being is a Buddha, or an ordinary person.

Adherents of Sōtō Zen may claim, 'Didn't the Buddha say, and was it not repeated by all the great masters over and over again, that each and every human being from the beginning possesses *buddha-nature* or, to be more precise, *is buddha-nature*' So what is all this striving for enlightenment good for, if awakening has "always already" been our essential nature? Thus, we do not practise *zazen* to reach some kind of goal, but we simply manifest by "nothing but aptly sitting" what we have been all along – *buddha-nature*!' In saying so, the adherents of Sōtō Zen emphasize the other aspect of non-dual truth, what in Buddhism is called *paramārtha satya* or 'absolute truth'.

Now, we should not fall into what we could call the

'relative-absolute-fallacy', which has been responsible for so many misunderstandings and so much dissent on the 'spiritual scene' of our days, and not *only* our days. This fallacy consists in either indiscriminately mixing up statements made from the point of view of these two clearly distinguishable aspects of the truth, ('discrimination' is valued highly in Buddhism for a very good reason) or in setting these aspects up against each other as irreconcilable contradictions. What we might call, 'ultimate truth', if naming it would not mean slandering it, consists of *both* aspects being one, or rather 'not-two', *simultaneously*. As the 'Heart Sūtra' says: 'Form as such is emptiness; emptiness as such is form.'

But somebody who only parrots the correct solution of a mathematical problem, without knowing and understanding the correct procedure of reaching this solution, is no real mathematician. And somebody who only parrots insights into absolute or even ultimate truth without having experienced this dimension of enlightenment himself is no authentic Buddhist, and even less a true Zen Buddhist. The clinging to semiskilled truths by 'people of lesser capacity', the indulgence in *opinions* that are based on the authentic insights of the 'creative geniuses', without really having comprehended these insights through one's own direct experience, has also in

Sōtō Zen led to a decline, a 'conceptualization' and departure from life and experience. This is comparable to the decline brought about by mechanized *kōan* practice. By the way, it is exactly this fallacy which is quite obvious in much of the writings of the proponents of the present-day 'Neo-Advaita fad', who tend to emphasize only the 'absolute' side of the medal of reality in a rather dualistic fashion.

For present-day Zen practitioners it is important to recognize and to beware of the dangers of a one-sided enhancement of the provisional concepts that characterize the two existing branches of Zen Buddhism. They should rather realize that *both* traditions are 'right' *and* 'wrong' simultaneously, and they should use for their own good whatever authentic insights and practices they find in *both* traditions.

ZEN AND THE DUALISTIC CONSCIOUSNESS OF THE OCCIDENT

Nowadays one already finds a number of Zen monasteries, hundreds of Zen centres and hundreds of thousands of 'adherents' of Zen in the Western world. But we dare say that it is not yet decided whether the Treasury of the Eye of the True Dharma on its way to the East, from India to China to Korea and Japan and from Japan during the past decades, to America and to Europe, will *really* arrive in the occident and take root in the consciousness of Western people.

In the West, the 'Transmission of the Light' encounters its greatest challenge so far. In East Asia, where the 'typical' Chan and Zen developed, this process took place within the framework of cultures, in which spiritual training, and the moral and ethical foundations of this training, belonged (other than in the West) to the highest values of these cultures. Thus, practitioners of Zen did not have to swim, all the time, against the mainstream of their socio-political environment. And what is even more decisive is that in these cultures the overall consciousness of the people was by far less dualistic than the consciousness of the 'fall of man', that is characteristic of those Mediterranean cultures which produced Judaism, Christianity and Islam. Brigitte D'Ortschy (Kōun-an Chikō Rōshi), was a contemporary Zen master who, coming from the West, knew and saw through, Western consciousness better than many Asian teachers. She made the point that this deeply dualistic occidental consciousness has an almost 'diabolic' (from the Greek *dia-bállein*, 'to disunite') tendency, sneakingly and almost imperceptibly, to turn all well-meant spiritual aspirations into their blatant opposite.

The history of the Christian Church (and of course of other institutionalized religions) is full of examples of this tendency. And the still very young history of Zen (and other Eastern traditions) in the West, is already overshadowed by guru hype, commercial interests, disunity among sects and schools and quite a number of lesser and greater scandals. If, as some concerned observers of the development of the Eastern traditions in the West recently have remarked, Zen in the West is in danger of dying even before it has really been born, this may be due (among other factors) to two tendencies, one Western and one Eastern, that we will briefly touch upon.

The Western tendency is its typical impatience, the sometimes all-too-hasty attempt to adapt Eastern traditions to the West. It is beyond all question that the cultural and ritual superstructures of Eastern traditions have to change, if these traditions are supposed to become *living* traditions, and not just exotic museum pieces, in the West. But in this process of assimilation the *essence* must not be lost. The 'absolute truth' that needs to be realized on the path of Zen, (also on the path of what D T Suzuki called 'democratic Zen') is also an 'absolute ruler'. That means 'truth' cannot be voted upon by the majority of the members of a community, and those 'truths' that *are* agreed upon in a democracy by vote, tend to be the 'lowest common denominator', the seemingly most convenient and least painful way of doing things. But smugness and convenience are the death of spiritual aspiration in general, and of the path of Zen in particular which demands our utmost commitment, even if that may seem uncomfortable to our ego.

And to the Eastern tendency – most Zen lineages active in the occident today have come to the West from Japan, and there is a deeply ingrained character trait of Japanese people, that also may prove problematic in the transmission of Zen to the West. As the modern Japanese philosopher and cultural critic Katō Shuichi has pointed out, the origins of the general psyche of the Japanese people are to be found in the social structures of the closely-knit communities of the small Japanese rice-growing villages of old. They used to be relatively isolated and independent of the rest of the world. For reasons that we cannot delve into here in detail, the members of these communities used to regard 'outsiders' (in Japanese *gaijin*, which today also means 'foreigners') with both adoration and with contempt.

This position with regard to 'gaijin' is often still obvious in the psyche of modern Japanese people. It may manifest itself as a sometimes unjustified high regard for the motivation of foreigners who come to them to study Zen, a high regard, which may be heightened all the more if these foreigners happen to have a position in a Western religious institution. This uncritical high regard can, in the process of Zen training, veil the possibility that not each and every 'religious' person from the West, may approach Eastern traditions and their masters out of the single motivation of abandoning *all* conditioning, and the superstructures of the Western religious institutions, as well as a rampant Western ego.

If out of this adoration students from the West are confirmed prematurely as Zen teachers and *dharma* heirs, this may not only be an expression of high regard, but also of the complementary 'contempt' for *gaijin*. A degree of inner maturation which may not be accepted as sufficient qualification for the inheritance of the Treasury of the Eye of the True Dharma even in quite advanced Japanese Zen disciples, may on the side of an occidental student be considered '*good enough for the West*'. If we keep in mind the motto of the ancient masters, that the insight of the disciple should surpass that of the master for the lineage not to degenerate, we will be sensitized to the necessity to maintain the high standards of the Zen of the Patriarchs with regard to transmission, if Zen is meant to be more than a passing New Age fad in the West.

Even if the motivation on both sides is nothing but the best, and driven by the well-meant intent to 'spread the *dharma*' and to bring the priceless tradition of Zen to the West, this strictness is all the more necessary. The germs of the decay of any 'spiritual culture', which have been accounted for and denounced by the sages and enlightened ones of all cultures and ages, contrary to the 'feel good spirituality' of the New Age, which regards all critique as 'un-spiritual', find a most conductive climate for growth in the West. One of the parasites that, on the soil of the occident, may prove especially dangerous for the survival of the still very tender sprout of Western Zen, is what Kōun-an Chikō

Rōshi used to call 'secondary aims'. In as much as we are allowed to speak of an 'aim' at all in Zen practice, that is from the point of view of relative truth, this aim is, by definition of the famous stanza attributed to Bodhidharma, 'the realization of one's own nature and being Buddha oneself'.

Ever since the beginnings of the preoccupation of Western treasure hunters with Zen, there has been an inclination to 'instrumentalize' this tradition, which in its essence eludes all reification. Zen in the occident is often mistaken as a mere 'method' and misused as a means to an end, in line with an approach that the contemporary Tibetan master Chögyam Trungpa has called 'spiritual materialism'.

This end may be outright lucre, as in countless books, seminars and workshops, which for example sell 'Zen' as a success formula for entrepreneurs, managers, stockbrokers or aspiring millionaires etc. The end may have a therapeutic nature – Zen as the magic pill against neurosis, depression and the like, Zen as a path to a 'cool', harmonic, well-adjusted lifestyle, Zen as a kind of spiritual Prozac. The end may be physical or mental peak performance as in certain martial arts (that have become more like 'martial sports') which often use Zen philosophy, more as a kind of exotic embellishment than as the primary ground of their practice. Zen may be marketed as a means for managing a 'stressful modern life' in a serene and equanimous way, by 'meditative training'. The aim can be, often unconsciously, the building up and maintaining a 'spiritual ego', the conviction that one is an especially spiritual, holy, illustrious human being that is superior to the common mob. The end can also be an attempt to drip-feed an ailing religious establishment with some 'oriental medicine' or to make an institution like the Christian Church more attractive to modern-day spiritual seekers by including meditation techniques gleaned from Zen, in the range of products on offer. The end could be conceived in terms of extremely noble, lofty, almost heroic motives, against which nobody could really have any objections – to save the world, to fight for a healthy environment, to counteract social injustice, to stand up against poverty or for people who are discriminated against and marginalized in our society.

Thus today we have Business Zen, Therapy Zen, Warrior Zen, Wellness Zen, 'Christian' Zen, Socially Engaged Zen, Ecology Zen, Feminist Zen, Gay Zen, Lesbian Zen, Street Zen, Prison Zen, Concentration Camp Zen, This-and-That Zen and all kinds of 'Zen Arts'. Only 'Zen in the Art of Picking Your Nose' has not – yet – been propagated!

But what about the Zen of the Patriarchs? Is it not 'attractive' enough for people of our day and age? Linji once said about the climate that prevailed in the monastery of his master Huangbo: 'Everywhere else people are cremated; here we bury them alive.' But the statement 'Here you will be robbed of everything that is dear and precious to you!' is not an advertising slogan likely to lure people from the comfort zone of their 'insurance policies'. That may be the reason why the goods offered by many Western Zen monasteries and Zen centres are looking more and more like the programme of a spiritual holiday camp. Certainly nobody wants to 'work' on his Zen vacations, and for all those who find it much too boring to sit around and do nothing all day, entertainment and diversions are offered, anything from 'meditative hiking' to Zen archery. For those who would rather pamper their 'wellness' than 'die on the cushion', exotic sideshows are on offer, from shiatsu or macrobiotics to neurolinguistic programming. And for those who feel they have not yet filled their minds with enough ideas, concepts, opinions and ideologies, there are lectures, discussion groups and 'sharing' sessions. Not to forget the possibility, afterwards, to continue the endless 'chatting' *about* Zen on the Internet.

Teishō or Lecture?

A 'lecture', which is meant to convey information that is objectified knowledge, should not be confused with the *teishō* of a Zen master, which is a 'presentation' of wisdom (*prajñā*). In a *teishō* the Zen master offers to the Buddha his genuine insight on a subject in the presence of the assembly of practitioners. While a lecture just feeds the intellect with concepts, the presentation of *prajñā* may touch the heart-mind of the hearer on a level beyond conceptualization, and may open it up for deeper insights.

No, no – there is nothing *wrong* with all of these activities in themselves. And from an absolute point of view (one that we have *realized* ourselves) all these activities are nothing else but a perfect manifestation of *buddha-nature*. And of course no Bodhisattva, be he on the path of Zen or on any other spiritual path, will look passively upon human suffering without doing her or his utmost to alleviate it. All secondary aims become problematic only when they thrust themselves into the foreground, and little by little become more important than the primary aim of Zen, and any other form of

Buddhism – awakening. Only on the foundation of this awakening can there be authentic 'Bodhisattva work'. And was it not the Awakened One who set out to overcome human suffering, and did he not show by his own example that suffering (our own and that of all sentient beings) *after all* can only be overcome by awakening?

No amount of Zen practice can guarantee or 'bring about' a *kenshō* or satori. Nevertheless (and this is one of the paradoxes of the Zen experience) a breakthrough seldom happens without the previous engagement of what is called *jiriki* or 'self power'. It is ones own 'meditative effort' (another paradox!) that prepares the Zen adept's field of consciousness for a breakthrough. This happens more like a kind of grace, by what is called *tariki* or 'other power', rather than as effect of the cause of *zazen*. Of course this is the description of the 'process of awakening' (a third paradox!) from the relative point of view; from the absolute point of view there is no 'self' or 'other', and no 'process'. Secondary aims are so problematic since, as we have seen, it is such an exacting and demanding task to cultivate the field for the realization of this awakening. And to engage oneself for a 'noble cause' can become one of the most ingenious tricks of our most dangerous enemy, 'we have met the enemy, *and it was us*!' It can become a clever way of avoiding the crucial sacrifice, namely ourselves, when we are convinced of already leading such a deeply 'spiritual' life.

THE RADICAL APPROACH OF ZEN

As Shākyamuni, the searcher, had to realize himself, to *really* alleviate suffering – one's own and the suffering of all sentient beings – radical means are necessary, that is, means that go to the root of suffering and cut it off. As the Buddha formulated in the 'Four Noble Truths' in his very first presentation of his insight after his Great Awakening, the root and deepest cause of suffering is the attachment and craving that arise out of a dualistic view of the world. And as he taught, there *is* a path to overcoming suffering, and this path is the 'Noble Eightfold Path'.

Buddha's 'Four Noble Truths'

1. All existence is painful and unsatisfactory. Birth, sickness, and death is suffering; coming together with what one does not like is suffering; separating from what one does like is suffering and the Five Aggregates (*skandhas*), which constitute the human personality, are suffering.
2. The cause of suffering is craving, the thirst for sensual pleasure, for becoming, and for passing away is suffering.
3. Suffering can be brought to an end by remainderless elimination of craving, the source of suffering.
4. The means for eliminating the cause of suffering is the Noble Eightfold Path.

The Noble Eightfold Path

1. Right View
2. Right Resolve
3. Right Speech
4. Right Conduct
5. Right Livelihood
6. Right Effort
7. Right Mindfulness
8. Right Concentration

Now 'right' or 'perfect' concentration (Sanskrit: *samyak samādhi*) which culminates in the 'four absorptions' or *dhyānas*, the central practice of Zen, is the eighth step of the Eightfold Path, its apex and *ultima ratio*. It must be emphasized, however, since this is often overlooked, especially in the West – that this pinnacle of the pyramid of the Eightfold Path cannot be realized and lived authentically without the stable foundation of the intellectual, moral and ethical perfection by the other seven dimensions of the Eightfold Path. And beyond this, we must not forget what the Buddha also emphasized: Any spiritual 'method' is only a raft that may take us to the 'other shore' (enlightenment) where, once we arrive, we must leave the raft behind. There would be no point in carrying the raft on our backs on our way into the mountains, as it has served its purpose. The 'provisional skilful means' of religion and spiritual training would thus, like the raft, become an obstruction to authentic living, or what Zhuangzi, one of the forefathers of Zen, called 'free and easy wandering'.

Thus, once again, what about genuine Zen, the Zen of the Patriarchs, in the West? As Kōun-an Chikō Rōshi once said: 'In the end there is no "genuine" Zen in contrast to fake Zen, as there is no "genuine" butter in contrast to "fake" butter. Butter is genuine butter and margarine is genuine margarine, and some people may prefer margarine to butter.' Likewise a certain practice is either genuine Zen, the Zen of the Patriarchs, *or it is no Zen at all*. It may then be something else, concentration training, psychotherapy, sports, pastime, ego trip, and the like, and this something else may be very useful and valid in itself, but it is not ZEN.

In the words of the Sixth Patriarch:

There is nothing to be taught,

nothing to be transmitted.

It is just a matter of seeing

one's own nature.

To talk about food does not fill your belly,
To talk about clothes does not keep you warm.
To satisfy your hunger you must have a meal,
To escape the cold you must have clothes to wear.
But you cannot detach from pondering and scrutinizing,
And from asserting that to follow Buddha is impossible.
Turn your gaze into your heart and at once you are Buddha –
You will never find him outside of yourself!

Hanshan,
'Poems from Cold Mountain'

ENDNOTES

1 Chan originated in China, but in the West it became known mainly in its Japanese form and reading as 'Zen'. So when we speak about this form of spiritual training in general, we use the word 'Zen', while 'Chan' refers specifically to the original Chinese manifestation.

2 *The Zen Teaching of Huang Po on the Transmission of Mind*, rendered into English by John Blofeld (Chu Ch'an), London (The Buddhist Society) 1968, p.35

3 *The Record of Transmitting the Light*. Zen Master Keizan's Denkōroku, translated by Francis H Cook, Los Angeles (Center Publications) 1991, p.32

4 *Wandering on the Way: Early Taoist Tales and Parables of Chuang Tzu*, translated with an Introduction and Commentary by Victor H Mair, New York (Bantam Books) 1994, pp.19–20

5 *Fung Yu-lan: A History of Chinese Philosophy*, Vol. II, 'The Period of Classical Learning', Princeton (Princeton University Press) 1953, p.266

6 ibidem, p.267

7 ibidem, p.268

8 *Wandering On the Way: Early Taoist Tales and Parables of Chuang Tzu*, translated with an Introduction and Commentary by Victor H Mair, New York (Bantam Books) 1994

9 *The Diamond Sutra and The Sutra of Hui Neng*, translated by A F Price and Wong Mou-Lam, Berkeley (Shambhala) 1969, pp.23–4

10 ibidem, p.37

11 *The Platform Sutra of the Sixth Patriarch*, the text of the Tun-huang manuscript, translated by Philip B Yampolsky, New York (Columbia University Press) 1967, p.127

12 *The Platform Sutra Of The Sixth Patriarch*, The Text of the Tun-Huang Manuscript with Translation, Introduction, and Notes by Philip B Yampolsky, New York (Columbia University Press) 1967, p.128

13 Translated from: *Hui-neng: Das Sutra des Sechsten Patriarchen*, German translation with commentary by Soko Morinaga Rōshi by Ursula Jarand, Bern, München, Wien (O W Barth) 1989, pp.39–40

14 In some versions of this text it is three years.

[15] Translated by R H Blyth in *Zen and Zen Classics*, Tokyo (Hokuseido Press) 1960, p.72

[16] This is just to make the point here, a rather superficial interpretation of 'no "Ho!" at all'. In a deeper sense, which certainly is more in accordance with Linji's mind, this last category can also be understood as a completely intent-less 'Ho!' – and thus as the highest form of this shout.

[17] From the forty-fascicle *Avatamsaka*, Fas. XXXII; quoted after D T Suzuki: *Essays in Zen Buddhism*, Second Series, London (Rider) 1985, p.19–20

[18] The first, the third and the fourth example are quoted from *The Gateless Barrier*, translated with a Commentary by Robert Aitken, Berkeley, California (North Point Press) 1991; transcription of Chinese names adapted.

[19] D T Suzuki, *Essays in Zen Buddhism*, Second Series, London (Rider) 1985, p.34

[20] ibidem, p.30

[21] *The Gateless Barrier*, op. cit., pp.8–9

[22] D T Suzuki, *Essays in Zen Buddhism*, op. cit., p.90

RESOURCES

For somebody who wants to practise Zen herself, the search for an *authentic* master of the Zen of the Patriarchs usually is his/her first trial on the path. This trial will show, whether he/she possesses 'appreciation of value', a kind of intuitive competence that is an indispensable prerequisite for finding the treasure. As in the case of the evaluation of a work of art, there are no 'objective' criteria for the evaluation of a master or a community. The searcher is thrown back on his or her capacity to recognize authenticity without being swayed by the opinions and preferences of others. The Daoist sage Laozi already said: 'The sage wears a coarse cloth on top, and carries jade within his bosom.' Accordingly the size of a monastery or Zen centre, the 'Far Eastern' air of the ceremonies and the loudness with which 'masters' and centres advertise themselves on the spiritual supermarket of our day, is often inversely proportional to the authenticity of the content conveyed, and the depth of Zen experience of the respective 'Zen teachers'.

The following addresses can be helpful when you are searching a Zen centre in your area:

http://iriz.hanazono.ac.jp/zen_centers/country_list_e.html

http://www.Buddhanet.info/wbd/index.php

http://www.dmoz.org/Society/Religion_and_Spirituality/Buddhism/Lineages/Zen/Centers/

http://zen.buddhism.org/zen-country.html

http://www.mbzc.org/centers.php4

http://www.sotozen-net.or.jp/kokusai/kokusai.htm

http://www.dharmanet.org/listings/

http://www.americanzenteachers.org/list.html

http://www.chan1.org/alinks.html

SELECTED BIBLIOGRAPHY OF WORKS IN ENGLISH LANGUAGE

There are magnificent works by Korean and Japanese Zen masters and quite a few remarkable books by Western Zen students; but since this book has concentrated on the Golden Age of Zen in China, this bibliography concentrates on books relevant to that same period. The readers who have approached the gate of the Zen tradition through the root writings of the masters of Chan, will find their way easily to the rest of the literature from the many branches of the Zen tradition that in the meantime have spread throughout the world.

Blyth, RH *Zen and Zen Classics*, Volume One: From the Upanishads to Huineng, 1960; Volume Two: History of Zen, 1964; Volume Three: History of Zen (Nangaku Branch) 1970; Volume Four: Mumonkan, 1966; all Tokyo (The Hokuseido Press)

Book of Serenity [Congronglu], Translated and Introduced by Thomas Cleary, Hudson, NY (Lindisfarne Press) 1990

Ch'an and Zen Teachings, Edited, Translated and Explained by Lu K'uan Yü (Charles Luk), London (Rider & Company) First Series 1960, Second Series 1961, Third Series 1962

Chang, Chung-yuan, *Original Teachings of Chan Buddhism*, New York (Vintage Books) 1971

Conze, Edward, *Buddhist Wisdom Books: The Diamond and the Heart Sutra*, London (Unwin Paperbacks) 1988

Cultivating the Empty Field: The Silent Illumination of Zen Master Hongzhi, Translated by Taigen Daniel Leighton with Yi Wu, San Francisco (North Point Press) 1991

Dumoulin, Heinrich, *Zen Buddhism: A History*, Vol. 1, *India and China*, New York (Macmillan) 1988

Ferguson, Andrew, *Zen's Chinese Heritage*, Boston (Wisdom Publications) 2000

Fischer-Schreiber, Ingrid; Ehrhard, Franz Karl, and Diener, Michael S [Stephan Schuhmacher], *The Encyclopaedia of Eastern Philosophy and Religion: Buddhism, Hinduism, Taoism, Zen*, Boston (Shambhala) 1989

Fung, Yu-lan, *A History of Chinese Philosophy*, Vol. 2, *The Period of Classical Learning*, Princeton (Princeton University Press) 1983

Gateless Gate, Newly Translated with Commentary by Zen Master Kōun Yamada, Los Angeles (Center Publications), 1979

Master Yunmen: From the Record of the Chan Master 'Gate of the Clouds', Translated, Edited and with an Introduction by Urs App, New York (Kodansha International) 1994

Radical Zen: The Sayings of Jōshū, Translated with a Commentary by Yoel Hoffman, Brookline, MA (Autumn Press) 1978

Sayings and Doings of Pai-chang, Ch'an Master of Great Wisdom, Translated from the Chinese by Thomas Cleary, Los Angeles (Center Publications) 1978

Suzuki, D T, *Essays in Zen Buddhism*, First, Second and Third Series, London (Rider & Company) 1985

Swampland Flowers: The Letters and Lectures of Zen Master Ta Hui, New York (Grove Press) 1977

Tao: A New Way of Thinking, A Translation of the Tao Tê Ching [Daodejing] with an Introduction and Commentaries, by Chang Chung-yuan, New York (Harper & Row) 1975

The Blue Cliff Record, Translated from the Chinese *Pi Yen Lu* by Thomas and J C Cleary, Boulder (Prajñā Press) 1978

The Book of Nothing: A Song of Enlightenment: Sosan's [Sengcan's] hsin hsin ming [*xinxinming*], translated by Philip Dunn and Peter Jourdan, Kansas City, MO (Andrews McMeel) 2002

The Complete Works of Chuang Tzu [Zhuangzi], Translated by Burton Watson, New York (Columbia University Press) 1968

The Diamond Sutra and The Sutra of Hui-neng, Translated by A F Price and Wong Mou-Lam, Berkeley, CA (Shambhala) 1969

The Gateless Barrier, Translated and with a Commentary by Robert Aitken, Berkeley, CA (North Point Press) 1991

The Platform Sutra of the Sixth Patriarch, The Text of the Tun-huang Manuscript with Translation, Introduction, and Notes by Philip B Yampolsky, New York (Columbia University Press) 1967

The Record of Rinzai, Translated from the Chinese by Irmgard Schloegl, London (The Buddhist Society) 1975

The Record of Transmitting the Light: Zen Master Keizan's Denkōroku, Translated by Francis H Cook, Los Angeles (Center Publications) 1991

The Record of Tung-shan, Translated by William F Powell, Honolulu (University of Hawaii Press) 1986

The Recorded Sayings of Ch'an Master Lin-chi Hui-chao of Chen Prefecture, Compiled by his humble heir Hui-jan of San-sheng, Translated from the Chinese by Ruth Fuller Sasaki, Kyoto (The Institute for Zen Studies) 1975

The Recorded Sayings of Layman P'ang: A Ninth Century Zen Classic, Translated from the Chinese by Ruth Fuller Sasaki, Yoshitaka Iriya, Dana R Fraser, New York & Tokyo (Weatherhill) 1971

The Sutra of Hui-Neng, Grand Master of Zen, with Hui-neng's Commentary on the Diamond Sutra, Translated from the Chinese by Thomas Cleary, Boston & London (Shambhala) 1998

The Way and Its Power: A Study of the Tao Tê Ching and Its Place in Chinese Thought, by Arthur Waley, New York (Grove Press) 1958

The Wisdom of Laotse [Laozi], Translated, Edited and with an Introduction and Notes by Lin Yutang, New York (The Modern Library/Random House) 1948

The Zen Teaching of Bodhidharma, Translated and with an Introduction by Red Pine, San Francisco (North Point Press) 1998

The Zen teaching of Huang Po on the transmission of mind, Translated by John Blofeld, Boston (Shambhala) 1994

The Zen teaching of Hui Hai on sudden illumination; being the teaching of the Zen Master Hui Hai, known as the Great Pearl; rendered into English by John Blofeld, London (Rider & Company) 1962

Three Chan Classics: The recorded sayings of Linji. Wumen's gate. The faith-mind maxim, Berkeley, CA (Numata Center for Buddhist Translation and Research) 1999

Transmission of Light [Denkōroku]: Zen in the Art of Enlightenment, By Zen Master Keizan, Translated with an Introduction by Thomas Cleary, San Francisco (North Point Press) 1990

Two Zen Classics: Mumonkan and Hekiganroku, Translated with Commentaries by Katsu Sekida, New York, Tokyo (Weatherhill) 1977

Upāsaka Lu K'uan Yü (Charles Luk), *The Transmission of the Mind Outside the Teaching*, London (Rider & Company) 1974

Wandering on the Way: Early Taoist Tales and Parables of Chuang Tzu [Zhuangzi], Translated with an Introduction and Commentary by Victor H Mair, New York (Bantam Books) 1994

Zen Comments on the Mumonkan by Zenkei Shibayama, Translated into English by Sumiko Kudo, New York (Harper & Row) 1974

Zen Letters: Teachings of Yuanwu, Translated and Edited by J C Cleary and Thomas Cleary, Boston & London (Shambhala) 1994